NATIONAL
HISTORY
B E E

HISTORY
snapsh○ts™

U.S. History 1900-1949

🌿 hexco

hexco

The average history textbook is a wealth of information, but often includes almost too much for quick study – leaving students to sieve through lines of text to understand the foundation of the issue at hand. The goal of our *Snapshots* series is to give students key information in bite-sized and manageable pieces without losing the trivia element that makes history fun.

Disclaimer notice: The content of any history contest is not limited to the events in this book. Dates and facts have been verified by at least two reliable sources, however, we encourage you to contact us if any information contained in this book is historically inaccurate.

Printed in the United States of America
ISBN-13: 978-0-692-12127-6

First printing, 2018
Hexco Academic
P.O. Box 199
Hunt, TX 78024
www.hexco.com

Author - Keisha Bedwell
Consultant Editor - Michael R. Cude, PhD, Schreiner University
Editors - Shannon Ament, Beth Mader, Shannon Barker, David Winkleman,
    Nancy Barnard, Linda Tarrant, Jennifer King, and Noel Putnam
Internal Design & Cover - Shannon Ament & Jennifer King

ORDERING INFORMATION
Special discounts are available on quantity purchases by schools, teams, corporations, associations, etc. For details, contact the publisher at the address above. Bookstores and wholesalers interested in resale options for this publication or *History Essentials* are encouraged to contact Hexco at (800) 391-2891, or email hexco@hexco.com.

There is a mysterious cycle in human events. To some generations much is given. Of other generations much is expected. This generation of Americans has a rendezvous with destiny.

– Franklin D. Roosevelt

CONTENTS

CHAPTER 1
Turn of the Century
1900-1909

CONTEXT

By the turn of the 20th century, the 300-year period of expansion across the North American frontier had come to a close. The West was won and Native American groups were overcome, then forced to assimilate and move to reservations. The continent was settled from coast to coast, and the nation entered a period of dramatic growth and change.

The U.S. was on the road to becoming a global superpower. Technological innovations enabled large-scale farming, allowing the nation to become the globe's forerunner in agricultural production. Industrial growth abounded as new technology made way for the construction of transcontinental railroads, oil wells, steel industries, and the mass production of automobiles. Mass production and industrial growth also laid the foundation for a consumerist society. Urban areas grew. Electrical lighting began to light up cities. Telephones were widely used, and motion pictures were a modern curiosity, while the concept of radio was on its way.

The promise of opportunity attracted many immigrants between 1880 and 1920. These immigrants passed through checkpoints like Ellis Island and Angel Island and often moved to urban centers like San Francisco, New York City, Chicago, and Boston. Unlike previous waves of immigrants to the continent who were from Western Europe and typically well-educated, many of these hailed from Southern and Eastern Europe and represented increasingly diverse cultures. Conditions in the U.S. were often an improvement for these immigrants. Many took low-paying, unsafe jobs and lived in slum-like conditions.

Progressives sought social and political reform to address issues often related to the fast pace of urban and industrial growth. Investigative journalism would come to characterize the Progressive Era. Corruption and unfair practices in politics, economics, and industry were exposed.

ELECTIONS & PRESIDENTS

Election of 1900

Incumbent and Republican candidate William McKinley defeated Democratic candidate **William Jennings Bryan**. This election took place after the Spanish-American War (1898), during which the U.S. secured Cuba's independence from Spain and gained overseas territories. Thus, the topic of U.S. expansionism turned out to be one of the election's key issues. McKinley garnered 292 electoral votes, while Bryan received a total of 155. Theodore Roosevelt served as McKinley's vice president.

William McKinley

William McKinley
1843-1901

McKinley was born and raised in Ohio. He was employed as a schoolteacher before enlisting and serving in the Union Army during the Civil War. After the war, he studied and practiced law and became involved in Ohio politics, first serving as a member of Congress and then as the state's governor. McKinley (Republican) ran for the presidency in the Elections of 1896 and 1900, defeating William Jennings Bryan (Democrat) both times. He was the 25th president, and his administration was focused on foreign policy. Some of his chief accomplishments while in office included raising protective tariffs intended to support American industry and winning the Spanish-American War. His second and final term was cut short in 1901, when a gunshot wound received from an anarchist at the Pan-American Exposition led to his death.

McKinley assassinated • September 6, 1901

President McKinley was gunned down by an anarchist named **Leon Czolgosz** at the Pan-American Exhibition. Gangrene set in and, as a result, the wound proved to be fatal. The nation's vice president, Theodore Roosevelt, was sworn in to replace him. McKinley's murderer was sentenced to death by electric chair.

Theodore "Teddy" Roosevelt

Theodore "Teddy" Roosevelt 1858-1919

Teddy Roosevelt hailed from New York. After graduating from Harvard, he pursued a career as a writer and politician. Even at this juncture in his political career, Roosevelt combatted the corruption of political machines and was concerned about the environment. During the Spanish-American War, he organized a volunteer cavalry known as the **Rough Riders** and fought with them in Cuba. When he returned to the U.S., he was backed by Thomas C. Platt, New York's Republican Party boss, and elected the governor of New York in 1898. While serving as governor, he combatted the corruption of corporations. He angered Platt and other political bosses, so they helped secure him the Republican vice presidential nomination in order to place him in a "powerless" position. McKinley and Roosevelt won the election, but the political bosses' maneuver backfired when McKinley died and Roosevelt ascended to the presidency. In true Progressive fashion, Roosevelt believed in a strong executive and used his "**bully pulpit**" to address foreign affairs, problems between business, labor, and the American people, and the conservation of resources. He gained the reputation of being a "**trust-buster**" and won the Election of 1904, promising Americans a "**Square Deal**" between capital and labor. Roosevelt expanded the U.S. Navy and reorganized the Army, alongside adding the **Roosevelt Corollary**, which called for U.S. intervention in the Americas if necessary, to the Monroe Doctrine. His foreign policy was aggressive, and he adopted the African proverb, "speak softly and carry a big stick." Roosevelt also made way for the construction of the **Panama Canal**.

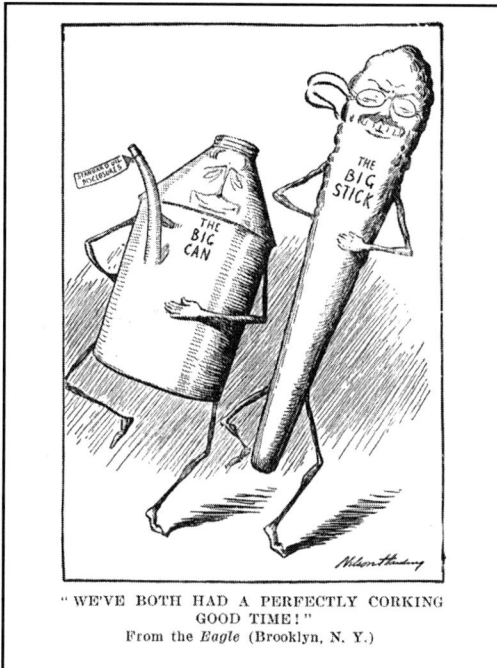

" WE'VE BOTH HAD A PERFECTLY CORKING
GOOD TIME! "
From the *Eagle* (Brooklyn, N. Y.)

Election of 1904

Republican candidate Theodore Roosevelt, who had acted as president since President McKinley's assassination, defeated the Democratic candidate Alton Parker. Roosevelt won by a landslide, defeating Parker by 336-140 electoral votes and garnering 56.4 percent of the popular vote. This was the first time in American history that someone who had originally ascended to the presidency without election retained the office by winning *their* first election.

Election of 1908

Incumbent President Theodore Roosevelt chose to not seek reelection and instead supported William Howard Taft. Taft won the Republican nomination, and William Jennings Bryan secured the Democratic nomination. Taft was victorious, defeating Bryan by 321-162 electoral votes to become the 27th president of the U.S.

William Howard Taft • 1857-1930

William Howard Taft

Taft was born in Cincinnati, Ohio, to a family with a background in law and politics. His family tree stretches all the way back to the Massachusetts Bay Colony, and his father was Ulysses S. Grant's secretary of war and attorney general. Taft himself graduated from his father's alma mater, Yale, and then the University of Cincinnati College of Law. He went on to practice law, serve as a judge, and hold several political appointments, including an appointment as governor-general of the Philippines by President William McKinley and as President Teddy Roosevelt's secretary of war. Roosevelt offered to endorse him as the Republican presidential candidate in the Election of 1908 or appoint him chief justice of the Supreme Court. While many children dreamt of being a fireman or a teacher, young Taft had always wanted to become a member of the Supreme Court. Due to encouragement from his wife, Helen Herron Taft, he reluctantly ran for president and served one term from 1909 to 1913. Though originally a friend of Teddy Roosevelt and a progressive Republican, he became increasingly aligned with the conservative branch of the party during his term in office. A split within the Republican Party during the Election of 1912 resulted in Taft's defeat by Woodrow Wilson (Democrat). Taft went on to teach law at Yale and serve as the tenth U.S. chief justice from 1921 to 1930, appointed by President Warren G. Harding. He remains the only president to have held a Supreme Court seat.

FOREIGN RELATIONS

Foraker Act • 1900

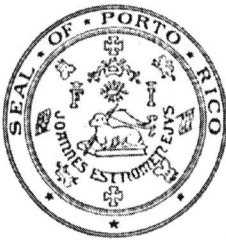

The 100-day-long Spanish-American War (1898) began and ended during McKinley's presidential administration. The U.S. defeated the Spanish and annexed Puerto Rico from Spain. The Foraker Act, named for its sponsor Joseph Benson Foraker, was signed by President McKinley and established a civilian government for Puerto Rico.

Platt Amendment • 1901

The U.S. occupied Cuba in 1898 as a result of the Spanish-American War. Before the war, the U.S. had promised Cuban independence. This amendment to an Army bill dictated the conditions under which the U.S. would end its occupation and guide its future relations with Cuba. It stipulated that Cuba could not create a treaty that might hurt its independent status or garner a large debt, among other things, or the U.S. would send troops. It also gave the U.S. the right to establish a naval base in Cuba at **Guantanamo Bay**. This amendment was stitched into the Cuban constitution and infringed on Cuban sovereignty. Though Elihu Root, U.S. secretary of war, was the primary drafter of this document, it was named for the Connecticut senator who presented it to the Senate, Orville Platt.

Chinese Exclusion Act of 1902

The first major law restricting immigration to the U.S. was the Chinese Exclusion Act (1882). It prohibited the Chinese for 10 years and was extended for another 10 by the Geary Act (1892). In 1902, another extension was added. Other groups would later be targeted in the same fashion.

Panama Canal • 1903-1914

Panama Canal lock construction

Previous attempts to construct this Central American canal had proven disastrous. When Theodore Roosevelt became president, he set his mind on its completion. Roosevelt launched warships to help Panama gain its independence in 1903 and signed the **Hay-Bunau-Varilla Treaty** with the newly independent republic later that year. This treaty, coupled with 10 million dollars and an agreement to pay an additional $250,000 each year, paved the way for the U.S. to build the canal. Despite the threat of tropical diseases like malaria and yellow fever and inhumane working conditions, the canal was completed and opened on August 15, 1914. It connects the Atlantic and Pacific Oceans through the Isthmus of Panama. This waterway is important, dramatically shortening the voyages of ships and allowing for cheaper trade routes. Prior to the completion of the canal, vessels traveling between the East and West Coasts of the U.S. had to sail all the way around Cape Horn, which is located at the southernmost point of South America and dramatically lengthened journeys by sea. The U.S. controlled the canal until 1979, then presided over it with a Panama joint committee until 1999, when it was completely turned over to Panama.

Roosevelt Corollary • 1904

President Theodore Roosevelt added what came to be called the Roosevelt Corollary to the Monroe Doctrine (1823) in his State of the Union address. The Monroe Doctrine asked Europeans to cease expansion in the Western Hemisphere. At that point in time, the U.S. lacked the power to enforce the doctrine. The Roosevelt Corollary expanded on it, adding that the U.S. would intervene in Latin American affairs if unrest or wrongdoing occurred within the nation's next-door neighbors. The U.S. began enforcement of this policy in 1905 with its invasion of the Dominican Republic and, over the years, carved out a sphere of influence throughout the Western Hemisphere. This went hand-in-hand with Roosevelt's motto, "speak softly and carry a big stick." Latin Americans were angered by the interference.

Hague Convention • June 15-October 18, 1907

The first Hague Convention met in 1899. The second convened in 1907. It addressed the laws and customs of war, such as fair treatment of POWs and bans on chemical weapons. It was one influence of the League of Nations, which was created after WWI.

Great White Fleet launched • December 16, 1907

On this day, President Theodore Roosevelt and a crowd of onlookers watched an armada of 16 U.S. battleships head to the open sea. The battleships were divided into four squadrons and referred to as the "Great White Fleet." The mission of this steam-powered, steel battleship fleet was to make a 43,000-mile cruise around the world. After the Spanish-American War (1898), the U.S. had not only acquired the Philippines, Guam, and Puerto Rico but had also become a power player in international politics. As a result, Roosevelt stressed the importance of upgrading and expanding the U.S. fleet for the purpose of protecting American foreign interests. This fleet was intended to show the world that the U.S. was prepared for anything. In essence, it was Roosevelt's way of flexing muscle and showing off the United States' "big stick."

Photo # NH 106192 "Great White Fleet" leaving Hampton Roads, Virginia, to begin its cruise around the World

Copyright, Pictorial News Co., 1907
BATTLESHIP FLEET, LEAVING HAMPTON ROADS, 1907

CIVIL RIGHTS & COURT CASES

National Negro Business League • 1900

Booker T. Washington, an African-American spokesman and founder of the **Tuskegee Institute**, created this league in hopes of promoting "commercial, agricultural, educational, and industrial advancement...and the commercial and financial development of the Negro." Washington believed that, if African Americans attained economic success, full equal rights would naturally follow.

National Negro Business League (Booker T. Washington seated front center), 1909
North Carolina Digital Collection

Lochner v. New York • 1905

New York's Bakeshop Act limited the number of hours bakers could work to no more than 10 hours a day with a maximum of 60 hours per week and set sanitation standards. Joseph Lochner owned a small bakery. Most of his customers arrived early, so some of his employees slept in the back of the bakery overnight if they had worked late the previous day. Some of Lochner's employees worked more than 60 hours per week. Lochner was reported to the authorities and subsequently arrested. His attorney argued that the Bakeshop Act interfered with Lochner's right to run a business and make a living; it unconstitutionally curtailed his liberty. The court ruled for Lochner in a controversial decision, citing that New York had no grounds for creating a labor law that interfered with an employee's work schedule. It was a labor law that violated the 14th Amendment's protection of liberty. In this case, it was the liberty given to the employer and employee to set the terms of their working relationship. The justices focused on the limit to the hours a person could work and freedom of contract considerations. Their decision established that the number of hours worked did not affect the health of the worker or the quality of the product the business made. The decision made it more difficult to establish labor laws related to working conditions and child labor. Poor working conditions could be found throughout the nation, and many of the rising workers' organizations considered the courts to be on the side of the capitalists rather than the people.

NAACP founded • February 12, 1909

The National Association for the Advancement of Colored People (NAACP), founded on this date, was one of the first civil rights organizations in the U.S. It combatted civil rights issues, including the segregation of schools, by way of legal strategies. Over the years, its leadership has included men like Booker T. Washington and W.E.B. Du Bois. The NAACP is still active today and, according to its mission statement, works to "ensure the political, educational, social, and economic equality of rights of all persons and to eliminate race-based discrimination."

TECHNOLOGY, INNOVATIONS, & DISCOVERIES

Brownie camera

Brownie camera invented 1900

Can you imagine a universe without camera phones? The Brownie film camera was created and launched by the **Eastman Kodak Company**. It cost $1 and, for the first time, made cameras and photography accessible to the general public. Their introduction of removable roll film containers permitted consumers to take film from the camera to develop photographs. Prior to this, the entire camera had to be packaged and sent back to Eastman-Kodak for development.

Transatlantic transmission • 1901

Though he was not the first to conduct experiments with electromagnetic waves, the first wireless communication company was created by **Guglielmo Marconi** in 1897. He sent the first electromagnetic signal across the Atlantic in 1901. These waves were transmitted code composed of dots and dashes. It was not until 1906 that the human voice and music were transmitted. Reginald Fessenden, a Canadian, transmitted this communication from Brant Rock, Massachusetts.

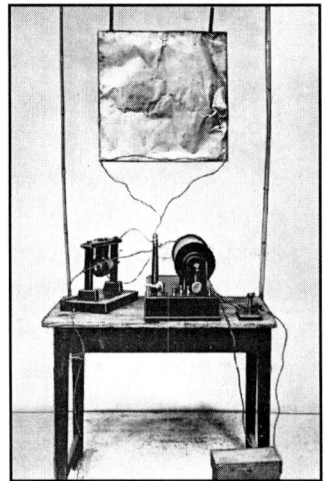

Marconi's first radio transmitter

Victrola • 1901

Thomas Edison invented the **phonograph**, a machine that both recorded and played sound, in 1877. The Victor Talking Machine Company, founded around 1901 by Eldridge Johnson, was the most successful maker of phonographs.

Nikola Tesla • 1856-1943

Tesla was born in Croatia in the Austro-Hungarian Empire but immigrated to the U.S. in 1884. The Serbian-American inventor was an engineer and is best known for his innovations in electrical power.

He worked for Thomas Edison's company before striking out on his own. Edison, now his rival, promoted the direct current system, and Tesla and George Westinghouse promoted the **alternating current** system. This U.S. conflict was called the "**War of the Currents.**" Edison's direct current was unable to transport electrical energy across long distances. Tesla's alternating current motor and electric systems are still used across the world today.

Nikola Tesla

Tesla was a visionary and a prolific inventor. Key inventions include the Niagara Falls hydroelectric power plant, the Tesla coil, fluorescent lights, laser beams, wireless communications, the remote control, and much, much more. He did not receive recognition for many of his achievements during his lifetime. Today, Tesla's birthday, July 10th, is celebrated as Nikola Tesla Day.

U.S. Steel • 1901

John Pierpont Morgan, a successful financier, and several other businessmen purchased Andrew Carnegie's steel company, merged it with other companies, and established the U.S. Steel Corporation in 1901. Through its ownership of all factors of production, this company was able to establish a monopoly on the American steel industry. As a matter of fact, this business was America's first billion-dollar company. J.P. Morgan was also involved in many other industries and projects, including the reorganization of U.S. railroads. In *United States v. United States Steel Corporation et al* (1920), the court ruled that the company did not violate the Sherman Antitrust Act, an act passed in 1890 that was the first to make monopolistic business practices illegal, despite that fact that it had nearly a 90 percent market share in the steel industry.

"Teddy" bear

Theodore Roosevelt was an adventurous spirit and an avid hunter. In 1902, the president went bear hunting in Mississippi with the state's governor. All members of this hunting party encountered a bear except Roosevelt. One man caught and secured a black bear to a tree and presented it to the president. Roosevelt said that it was unsportsmanlike to shoot the trapped creature, and newspaper coverage spread the story like wildfire. It inspired Morris

Clifford Berryman - *Washington Post*

Michtom and his wife Rose, candy shop owners, to design a stuffed animal called "Teddy's Bear." Roosevelt gave them his permission to create the namesake, and the toys sold like hotcakes.

Air conditioning

Can you imagine a world without air-conditioning? The basis for the modern air conditioner (and refrigerator) was developed by a Florida doctor, John Gorrie, in the 1840s. He created a machine that made ice via compression and cooled a room by blowing air above the ice. Gorrie's idea, however, never found financial backing. In 1902, **Willis Carrier** devised a machine that operated on a similar concept, blowing air over cold coils, and created the first air conditioning company. Carrier's company is still in operation today.

The Great Train Robbery • 1903

This short Western film is about a group of bandits who hold up a train and are tailed by a sheriff's posse. It was directed by Edwin S. Porter and includes a violent scene of a gun firing directly toward the camera which frightened viewers. It was one of the first movies to follow a narrative. During this era, motion pictures were silent.

4 CYL. MODEL T
FORD, 1908

Ford Model T

Ford Motor Company founded

In 1903, Ford Motor Company was established. **Henry Ford**, the man at the company's helm, released the **Model T** in 1908. This model became the first automobile that was both efficient and affordable for the general public. He accomplished this by implementing innovative methods of mass production, including building plants, using standard and interchangeable parts, and creating factory assembly lines. Fifteen million Model Ts would be produced. Model Ts were nicknamed "Tin Lizzies."

Nickelodeons

On June 19, 1905, Harry Davis premiered the first nickelodeon in Pittsburgh, Pennsylvania. Small theatres like this were called "Nickelodeons," because admission was a nickel. "Odeon" was the Greek word for "theatre." This was the first public movie theater on U.S. soil. Cinema would come to knock vaudeville entertainment from the limelight, and the era of film began.

Wright brothers' flight • December 17, 1903

On this date, **Wilbur** and **Orville** Wright took to the skies and successfully landed the first airplane flight in Kitty Hawk, North Carolina. This invention and its continual refinement throughout the century permitted humans to take to airspace for the first time. It was later adapted to carry freight and commercial passengers, as well as fight in World War I.

1904 Wright Flyer - Library of Congress

North Pole exploration • April 6, 1909

On this date, American explorers Robert E. Peary, Matthew Henson, and four Inuit men are believed to have reached the North Pole. Upon their return from the Arctic wilderness, they found that another American, Dr. Frederick A. Cook, had claimed to have reached the North Pole on April 21, 1908. There is still dispute regarding who was the first to reach the pole.

LITERATURE & JOURNALISM

Muckrakers • c. 1902-1912

"Muckraker" is a term used to describe American writers who sought to expose corruption in government and business and initiate reform. Muckraking evolved from yellow journalism, a form characterized by sensationalism, and included not only journalists, but novelists and reformers. It is primarily associated with the early 20th century, and the term was first coined by President Theodore Roosevelt. "Muckraker" is a reference to a character in *Pilgrim's Progress* by John Bunyan, and in his first usage of the term, Roosevelt explicitly referenced journalist William Randolph Hearst. Notable muckrakers include Upton Sinclair, Ida Tarbell, and many others.

Ida Tarbell's exposé • 1902-1904

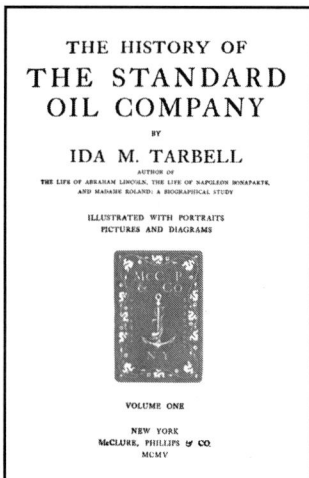

THE HISTORY OF
THE STANDARD
OIL COMPANY
BY
IDA M. TARBELL
AUTHOR OF
THE LIFE OF ABRAHAM LINCOLN, THE LIFE OF NAPOLEON BONAPARTE,
AND MADAME ROLAND: A BIOGRAPHICAL STUDY

ILLUSTRATED WITH PORTRAITS
PICTURES AND DIAGRAMS

VOLUME ONE

NEW YORK
McCLURE, PHILLIPS & CO.
MCMV

Volume one of Ida Tarbell's
magazine series

Tarbell was an editor and writer, as well as the daughter of a man whose small oil production company had been forced from business by John D. Rockefeller and Standard Oil. She wrote a 19-part series of magazines titled *The History of the Standard Oil Company*, in which she exposed Rockefeller's unethical business methods and evaluated his character. Her exposé infuriated the public and eventually led to the 1911 Supreme Court case, *Standard Oil Co. of New Jersey v. United States*. The court ruled that Standard Oil be broken up due to its violation of the Sherman Antitrust Act.

The Jungle • February 1902

Swift & Co.'s Packing House in Chicago, IL

A socialist writer named **Upton Sinclair** visited "Packington" in Chicago, Illinois. This visit to the Chicago meatpacking district moved Sinclair to pen a novel that not only criticized capitalism and the exploitation of labor but also revolutionized the American meat industry. Though Sinclair intended *The Jungle* to serve as an exposé of meat plant workers' horrible conditions, his description of the unsanitary and unsafe meat manufacturing process also led to the **Meat Inspection** and **Pure Food and Drug Acts** (1906). These acts were intended to prevent the adulteration and misbranding of consumer products. His novel became a prime example of successful muckraking, or investigative journalism, as it successfully moved both President Theodore Roosevelt and the general public to action.

While Sinclair's goal was to catalyze justice in unfair labor practice, the American public interpreted his novel as reason to improve the deplorable and unsanitary conditions found in slaughterhouses. Sinclair noted, "I aimed at the public's heart and by accident I hit it in the stomach." Trusts fought the expansion of government power, but the legislation was passed.

Theodore Dreiser • 1871-1945

Born in Indiana, Dreiser was the son of a German immigrant. He was an author and pioneered naturalism, or unswerving realism. One of the underlying focuses of his works was the social issues faced by a newly industrialized America. His first novel, and one of his most famous, was *Sister Carrie* (1900). Another key Dreiser work was *An American Tragedy* (1925).

L. Frank Baum • 1856-1919

Baum first gained popularity with *Father Goose, His Book* (1899) and became a best-selling children's author. He published *The Wonderful Wizard of Oz* in 1900 and went on to publish more books as part of the Wizard of Oz collection. These were later adapted into a Broadway musical and movie.

Jack London • 1876-1916

John Griffith Chaney, who adopted the name Jack London, was born in San Francisco and led an adventurous life. He was an author, journalist, socialist, world traveler, and much more. London was profoundly influenced by his experiences, such as his time seeking fortune in the Yukon during the gold rush. When he began writing in 1893, he pulled on these experiences to craft his novels. Many of his works address the struggle for survival. Some of his most popular novels include the books that catapulted him to fame, *The Call of the Wild* (1903) and *White Fang* (1906).

Edith Wharton • 1862-1937

Wharton, an author from New York, had a lengthy literary career. The central topic of many of her writings was upper-class society, a reflection of her own well-to-do background. Some of her best-known works include *The House of Mirth* (1905) and the *The Age of Innocence* (1920). She was the first woman to win a Pulitzer Prize.

Edith Wharton

William Randolph Hearst (1863-1951)

William Randolph Hearst

Hearst, the son of a gold mine owner and California senator, established an immensely successful newspaper chain name and altered the face of American journalism. Hearst and his *New York Journal* engaged in a serious rivalry with Joseph Pulitzer's *New York World*, giving rise to sensationalism, intense promotional schemes, yellow cartoons, and the term "**yellow journalism**." Hearst was actively involved in politics, and his newspaper chain was incredibly influential, effectively manipulating public opinion. As a matter of fact, its reporting incensed the public and pressured the government to wage the Spanish-American War (1898).

Edward Willis Scripps • 1854-1926

Scripps established a newspaper in 1878 and went on to become the first U.S. publisher to create and own a significant newspaper chain. He claimed his newspapers were written for the working people. Scripps and other newspaper owners joined to create the United Press in 1907. This international news syndicate competed with the Associated Press and still provides stories for newspapers and other media to purchase today.

Elmo Roper • 1900-1971

Roper was experienced in the field of marketing research, surveys, and public opinion. He took his experience and created the first scientifically styled poll to predict political outcomes. With this, he correctly predicted Franklin D. Roosevelt's presidential victories during three elections!

SPORTS

First Rose Bowl • January 1, 1902

Michigan, representing the East, and Stanford, representing the West, faced off at the Throop Polytechnic Institute (what is now the California Institute of Technology) in Pasadena, California. Michigan won 49-0, and eventually, a longstanding New Years' Day college football tradition was born.

First World Series • October 1-13, 1903

In 1903, the American League (AL) and the National League (NL) competed in a best-of-nine playoff series. The Boston Americans (representing the AL) defeated the Pittsburgh Pirates (representing the NL) and eventually came to be called the Boston Red Sox. The World Series, or annual post-season championship series, was established.

1903 Boston Americans - American League

SIGNIFICANT NAMES & EVENTS

Gold Standard Act • March 14, 1900

1928 gold standard one dollar bill

At this point in history, the Republican Party was the majority party in Congress, and William McKinley, also a Republican, was president. Republicans used their power to pass the Gold Standard Act. The gold standard required the U.S. government to fix its dollar holdings and exchange rate to gold. Their Democratic opponents had championed "free silver," or the use of silver in addition to gold to back American currency. This had been a big point of contention during the presidential Election of 1896.

Isaac's Storm • September 8, 1900

Galveston, the largest port city in Texas, was hit by a devastating Category 4 hurricane. Over 5,000 people lost their lives. As a result, Houston soon became Texas' leading port, and the city of Galveston raised the elevation of buildings and constructed a seawall. The storm is often called Isaac's Storm, after Isaac Cline, the chief of the Galveston U.S. Weather Service Bureau at the time. After the storm, Cline dedicated his life to the study of tropical cyclones.

Isaac's Storm, Galveston, Texas, 1900

Pelican Island National Wildlife Refuge • 1903

During the late 19th century, the fashion industry placed bird feathers in high demand. To meet this demand, bird populations were decimated. Concerned citizens and naturalists in Florida campaigned for the protection of non-game birds and were ultimately successful when President Theodore Roosevelt issued an executive order that established America's first national wildlife refuge in Pelican Island, Florida.

Roosevelt, a lifetime sportsman and hunter, was upset that the nation's big game, like bison and elk, were disappearing and sought to protect the country's wildlife and natural resources. During his presidency, he was an advocate for conservation, creating the United States Forest Service and championing the creation of numerous parks, sanctuaries, monuments, and preserves. There are more national parks dedicated to him than any other POTUS (six in total), and he is sometimes called the "conservationist president."

Great San Francisco Earthquake • April 18, 1906

View of aftermath and fires from Sacramento Street in San Francisco, 1906
Library of Congress

This earthquake had an estimated magnitude of 7.8 and caused immense amounts of damage along the San Andreas Fault and northern California's coastline. It triggered fires in San Francisco, its epicenter, and destroyed most of the city. Many perished. The state of California is located on this fault line, making earthquakes a common occurrence. This disaster allowed scientists to gather significant data about earthquakes, which helped them to better understand the phenomenon.

31

Oklahoma • November 16, 1907

On this date, Oklahoma became the 46th state. The state's name is derived from the Choctaw people's words for "people" and "red." This region had been acquired by the U.S. from Napoleonic France during the Louisiana Purchase in 1803, and the state was later carved from the Oklahoma Territory and Indian Territory.

Background: The government had forced many Native American groups to relocate to this area during the 19th century, but after the Civil War, white settlers desired land and people called "Boomers" illegally squatted in this area. Giving in to this pressure, the American government opened up this area to white settlement in 1889. Those who squatted illegally to get a jump on picking out the best land were called "Sooners," thus the state's official nickname, the "**Sooner State**." In 1907, Oklahoma Territory and Indian Territory were admitted as a state. Agriculture and oil production would come to be a significant part of this state's economy.

Portrait of Pablo Picasso by Jaun de Gris in the Cubist style - Art Institute of Chicago

Cubism • c. 1907-1914

This movement was begun in Paris by a Spanish artist named Pablo Picasso and Frenchman Georges Braque. Its name, Cubism, references their works' abstract geometric forms and was coined by an art critic named Louis Vauxcelles. Cubist artists did not believe art was required to imitate nature and played up two-dimensionality, depicting the objects of their paintings from different perspectives and breaking the objects of their paintings into geometric shapes.

Typhoid Mary

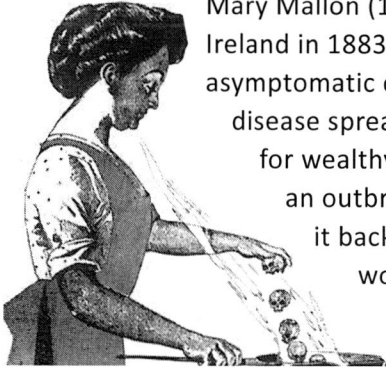

Mary Mallon (1869-1938) immigrated to New York City from Ireland in 1883. Though she appeared healthy, she was an asymptomatic carrier for typhoid fever, a highly contagious disease spread by bacteria. Mary was employed as a cook for wealthy families. After her employer experienced an outbreak, a freelance sanitary engineer tracked it back to Mary. Seven families she had previously worked for reported an outbreak of the disease. In 1907, she was quarantined by the New York City Health Department. She was released in 1910 on the provision that she cease working as a cook. In 1915, her employment as a cook at a maternity hospital in Manhattan resulted in 25 infections and two deaths. "Typhoid Mary" was quarantined yet again and remained there until her death, 23 years later. While she was not the only carrier of the disease or cause of all U.S. outbreaks, she is the most famous.

New York American Journal, June 20, 1909

Bureau of Investigation established • 1908

Urban growth was accompanied by a rise in criminal activity and violence. Ethnic tension, economic disparity, and the corruption of political machines and big business contributed to the growing crime rate. At this point in time, there were local (and some state) police forces with poor training and low pay, and there was nobody to enforce law across the great expanse of the nation. Charles Bonaparte, second attorney general during President Theodore Roosevelt's administration and, yes, Napoleon Bonaparte's grandnephew, expressed frustration that he had to borrow men from the Secret Service to investigate and create a case. When Congress banned their use, Bonaparte established his own group of agents to investigate for the Department of Justice. This organization later became the Federal Bureau of Investigation (FBI) we know today in March 1909.

Harry Houdini • 1874-1926

Harry Houdini performing an escape act

Ehrich Weiss, or "Harry Houdini," was born in Budapest, Hungary, and moved to Wisconsin as a young child. At the age of 18, he began to travel as a performing magician. His breakthrough came in 1899 when he met Martin Beck, who gave Houdini a chance and made him a big name in the **vaudeville** performing circuit. Vaudeville, a type of variety show, was popular entertainment at the turn of the century. Houdini was known for amazing escapes and magic tricks, which were often a combination of technical execution, illusion, and physical strength. Some of his most famous escapes included the "milk can escape," and the "Chinese Water Torture Cell." Houdini remained one of the globe's top performers until his death.

NOTABLES & TRIVIA

NOTABLE NAMES

Isodora Duncan

H.L. Mencken

Louis Henry Sullivan

At the turn of the century, feathers popularly adorned lady's hats.

Government restrictions on wild game birds caused manufacturers to turn to farmed animals, such as ostriches, in order to meet demand.

Independent Research:

How did Theodore Roosevelt expand the powers of the executive branch?

Giving Back

Andrew Carnegie, 1913 - Library of Congress

Wealthy industrialist Andrew Carnegie believed that the "well-to-do" should practice philanthropy and give back to society. A man of his word, he gave away most of his fortune. A portion of this money was used to build public libraries across the U.S. and even in the U.K., Australia, and New Zealand.

Interestingly enough, the U.S. executive's home was called the "Executive Mansion," "President's Palace," or "President's House" until Teddy Roosevelt began calling it the "White House" in 1901.

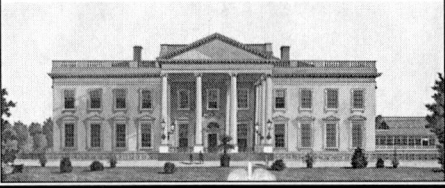

Which president's likeness can be found on the penny?

You guessed it — Abraham Lincoln. His image was added to the one-cent coin in 1909 and was the first American coin decorated with the portrait of a historical figure. It was done so in honor of the centennial of Lincoln's birth.

Between 1892 and 1954, Ellis Island was the primary entry point for the new wave of immigrants. Situated roughly a mile from Manhattan Island, it served as an immigration station. Some speculate that roughly 40 percent of today's American citizens are related to at least one person who passed through Ellis Island (including your author!)

Major Companies

Pepsi-Cola Company, 1902

General Motors Company, 1908

NOTABLE INNOVATIONS

Vacuum cleaner • 1901
First radio broadcast • 1906
Bakelite • 1907
Electric washing machine • 1909

CHAPTER 2
The Great War
1910-1919

CONTEXT

The Progressive Era continued. President Woodrow Wilson took the nation's helm in 1912 and remained there for the majority of the decade. Since the late 19th century, the nation had experienced significant urbanization and industrialization. This growth created new problems and spurred the government to reimagine its role.

The U.S. attempted to distance itself from European conflicts. This stance was challenged in the summer of 1914 when World War I (WWI) erupted in Europe between the Central Powers (Germany and Austria-Hungary) and the Triple Entente (Britain, France, and Russia). President Wilson declared neutrality. However, Britain's blockade interrupted U.S. trade with Germany between 1914 and 1916. As a result, Germany resorted to a policy of unrestricted submarine warfare targeting vessels aiding the Entente war effort. This impacted American trade. In the case of the *Lusitania*, Americans aboard a ship the Germans attacked were killed. This, combined with other instances of German aggression, incensed Americans.

The Zimmermann Telegram, an intercepted message, proved to be the last straw. This communication was sent by Germany to encourage Mexico to join the fight against the U.S. in return for the recovery of lands that had gone to the U.S. after the Mexican-American War. President Woodrow Wilson declared war in 1917.

The government called on the American people's patriotism and utilized propaganda and other methods to fund the war and garner the people's support for wartime efforts. Prior to WWI, the U.S. economy was in a state of recession. From 1914 to 1918, Europeans bought American goods and the U.S. economy boomed, creating factories and equipment that helped the U.S. prepare for wartime production. When the U.S. joined the Allies and the war in 1917, production and industry shifted from a focus on civilian goods to war goods. U.S. federal spending rose, and military and manufacturing employment opportunities caused unemployment to drop. The war was paid for by a combination of tax money, borrowing from the people and banks, and printing money. Americans purchased war bonds, also known as "liberty bonds," to help finance the war. The government had a hand in the economy, including price and production controls, which set the stage for future government intervention in times of crisis (like the Great Depression).

PRESIDENTS & ELECTIONS

Election of 1912
November 5, 1912

This election pitted the incumbent, Republican President William Howard Taft, against Democratic candidate and governor of New Jersey, Woodrow Wilson. The candidates debated the nature of government in the context of industrial growth and change. While Taft championed maintenance of the status quo and big business, Wilson was progressive, championing a "**New Freedom**" platform, and believed change was necessary.

THE LATEST ARRIVAL AT THE POLITICAL ZOO

Political cartoon, July 20, 1912 - *Harper's Weekly*

Some Republicans were dissatisfied with President Taft's conservatism and renomination. As a result, they formed the **Progressive Party** and nominated former president Theodore "Teddy" Roosevelt as its candidate. Unlike Taft, whom he had supported in the election of 1908, Roosevelt sought reform, and his program was called "New Nationalism." This party's nickname, the "**Bull Moose Party**," came from Teddy's description of himself as a man of vigor and strength. A fourth candidate and third proponent of progressive reform was **Eugene V. Debs** of the **Socialist Party**.

Taft and Roosevelt split the Republican vote, and Debs won almost 10 percent of the vote. Wilson was victorious by a landslide of electoral votes. He was the first president to have been born in the southern U.S. since the Civil War. This election is often cited as one of the most significant in American history.

Woodrow Wilson • 1856-1924

Woodrow Wilson

Wilson was born in Virginia and grew up in the South, witnessing both the Civil War and Reconstruction. Though he struggled with dyslexia as a child, he was an academic and graduated from the College of New Jersey (now known as Princeton) in 1879. He attended law school at the University of Virginia before going on to earn a doctorate in History of Government from John Hopkins University. Wilson taught at several universities, then at Princeton. By 1902, he was president of his alma mater and a champion of educational reform. Members of the Democratic Party noted the impact he had made at Princeton and convinced him to run for governor of New Jersey in 1910. He won and enacted progressive policies and combatted political machines. In 1912, he won the Democratic presidential nomination and the election. Wilson remained in office from 1913 to 1921. He implemented many reforms, including the Underwood-Simmons Tariff, the creation of the Federal Reserve System, and the Clayton Antitrust Act. At the onset of WWI, he adopted a policy of neutrality. He was reelected for keeping America out of WWI but was forced to enter the war when German aggression could no longer be ignored.

Election of 1916 • November 7, 1916

During his first term, incumbent Democratic candidate Woodrow Wilson enacted popular progressive legislation. He had also kept the U.S. neutral and out of World War I and campaigned with the slogan, "He kept us out of war." These policies helped him win a closely fought victory over the Republican candidate, **Charles Evans Hughes**.

Wilson incapacitated • October 2, 1919

Edith Wilson

President Woodrow Wilson suffered a severe stroke while traveling to promote the League of Nations. Thereafter, and until his death in 1924, he was disabled. As a result, Wilson could not continue to campaign for adoption of the League of Nations. Though the League was created, the U.S. opted to not join. The public was not made aware of the president's condition, and the First Lady, Edith Wilson, took on a number of her husband's roles.

WORLD WAR I

This section will discuss the war from the American perspective and address several key battles, but by no means all.

WWI begins in Europe • July 28, 1914

In light of Archduke Franz Ferdinand's assassination by a Serbian nationalist named Gavrilo Princip, Austria-Hungary, encouraged by Germany, declared war on Serbia. Russia rose to back its Serbian ally, a series of alliances were triggered, and the war began.

The primary Allied Powers included the British Empire, France, and Russia. Opposing them were the Central Powers, which primarily consisted of Germany, Austria-Hungary, and the Ottoman Empire. The U.S. would not enter WWI until 1917.

WWI Western Front trenches

Trench warfare

At the war's beginning, new weaponry included portable but powerful machine guns and rapid-fire field artillery. These were combined with man-made trenches and innovations like barbed wire and mines to create trench warfare. Frontal assaults by cavalry or infantry would be rendered suicidal in the wake of such weaponry. As a result, WWI was destined to become a long-lasting war of attrition. The combatants learned that attacks by sea and air could inflict harm from a distance more effectively, and innovations in these arenas were explored although the technology did not develop quickly enough to break the deadlock.

Unrestricted submarine warfare

U-boats were German submarines. Submarines were invented during an earlier period but were first fitted with diesel engines around 1912. The German policy of unrestricted submarine warfare was intended to break Britain's blockade. Any ship approaching England was considered a legitimate target if it was perceived to be helping the Allied war effort. This included civilian vessels, such as merchant ships, transporting supplies to the front. After limiting use of the tactic in light of U.S. threats, German military leaders reinstated the policy in 1917 in an effort break the deadlock. This gamble backfired when it helped lead the U.S. to enter the war.

Sinking of the *Lusitania* • May 7, 1915

The RMS *Lusitania* was a British ocean liner and the largest passenger ship of its day. On this voyage, it was also carrying munitions to the front. The ship was torpedoed and sunk by a German U-boat in the Atlantic Ocean off the coast of Ireland. Germany breached the international laws known as the **Cruiser Rules** by firing on a non-military vessel without warning. Nearly 1,200 people died, including over 100 Americans. This incident shifted American public opinion against Germany. The sinking of civilian vessels was to become one of the reasons that the U.S., a nation determined to stay out the European conflict, would enter the war two years later.

Zimmermann Telegram • 1917

This telegram proposed that Mexico support Germany if its upstairs neighbor, the U.S., elected to join WWI. The proposition offered Mexico monetary support and land it had lost to the U.S., including Texas, New Mexico, and Arizona territory, in return for its alliance to Germany. The message was sent by Arthur Zimmermann, Germany's foreign secretary, and its intended recipient was the Germany's ambassador to Mexico. It was intercepted by the British and given to the U.S. The telegram was published by newspapers nationwide and incensed the public.

U.S. enters WWI • April 6, 1917

After receiving both Congress' and the House of Representatives' approval to do so, President Woodrow Wilson declared war on Germany. The U.S. joined the Allied Powers, including Britain, France, Russia, and Italy, in their fight against the Central Powers, which included Germany, Austria-Hungary, the Ottoman Empire, and Bulgaria.

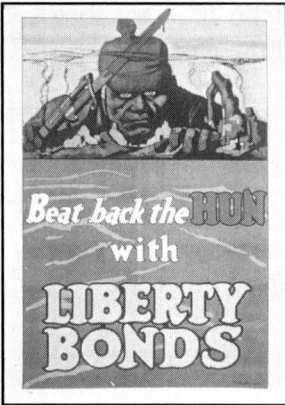

"Beat back the Hun with Liberty Bonds," by Fred Strothmann
National Archives

Committee on Public Information (CPI) • April 13, 1917

President Wilson created the CPI to motivate the American people to support the war effort after the U.S. shed its neutrality and joined WWI. He selected a muckraking journalist named **George Creel** to lead the CPI, which came to be known as the "Creel Committee." This organization created posters, films, news articles, billboards, speeches, and other pro-war and anti-German propaganda to promote the war effort.

U.S. Food Administration August 10, 1917

When the U.S. joined the Allies, President Wilson created the Food Administration and asked Herbert Hoover to head the organization. The Food Administration helped to feed not only American troops but also the Allies; Western Europe and its food supply had been destroyed by three years of warfare. While Europe had forcefully rationed food, Hoover encouraged the American people to voluntarily consume less and assist in his efforts by pulling on their compassion and patriotic heartstrings through advertising and educational programs. The efforts of the American people included altering their diets, participating in conservation programs like "Meatless Tuesdays" and "Wheatless Wednesdays," and planting victory gardens.

Impact of American entry

Prior to U.S. entry, the Allied effort was flagging. America not only contributed badly needed supplies but also a fresh and seemingly endless supply of soldiers that broke the deadlock in the war of attrition. The U.S. Department of War drafted and mobilized the U.S. First Army (**American Expeditionary Force**) with astonishing speed, and they fought in the final battles on the Western Front, known as the **Hundred Days Campaign**. These soldiers were led by General **John "Black Jack" Pershing** and, though they were not as battle-seasoned or tactically sophisticated as their European counterparts, their contribution convinced Germany to reach an armistice. The war ended by November of 1818.

Armistice of Compiègne • November 11, 1918

The Allies escorted the German delegation by railway for 10 hours across the war zone of Northern France. After placement aboard supreme Allied commander Ferdinand Foch's private rail train, they were taken to a secret location at a railway siding in the forest. Signed at 5 a.m. on November 11, 1918, this armistice went into effect at 11 a.m. Paris time. The event was referred to as the "eleventh hour of the eleventh day of the eleventh month." This agreement ended the fighting between Germany and the Allies and was named after the location where it was signed, the forest Compiègne, in France. Celebrated as Armistice Day, Veterans Day, or Remembrance Day in many countries, this annual tribute honors the dead.

Armistice Day celebration in Paris, November 11, 1918

Spanish Flu pandemic • 1918-1919

This pandemic, which occurred on the tail end of WWI and was spread across the globe by the movement of soldiers, was the deadliest in recorded history. Unlike most forms of influenza, its mortality rate was the highest for people between the ages of 20 and 40. It was also known as "La Grippe." Globally, an estimated 20 to 50 million perished.

Paris Peace Conference • 1919-1920

The fighting had come to an end, and peace negotiations began in Paris. The primary leaders, or "**Big Four**," at this conference were Woodrow Wilson (U.S. president), David Lloyd George (British prime minister), Georges Clemenceau (French prime minister), and Vittorio Emanuele Orlando (Italian prime minister). Peace negotiations of this scope were unprecedented, and these men met 145 times to craft the decisions.

President Wilson presented the **Fourteen Points**, which discussed territorial issues and provisions to maintain global peace, to the U.S. Congress. One facet of Wilson's vision was a **League of Nations** to govern international relations. This dream was not fully realized, as the U.S. did not adopt this provision of the Treaty of Versailles nor join the League of Nations after its creation.

Treaty of Versailles • June 28, 1919

At the Paris Peace Conference's end, German and Allied delegates signed the Treaty of Versailles. Other treaties dealt with the additional Central Powers on the German side of WWI. The Treaty of Versailles officially ended the war but planted seeds of resentment that would later lead to WWII. The limitations imposed on Germany were oppressive and humiliating. One of the articles of the treaty required Germany and its allies to accept full responsibility for all damages and losses that occurred during the war. The other members of the Central Powers signed separate treaties that contained similar wording. This opening article of the reparations section,

Article 231, was called the **War Guilt Clause**. The treaty required Germany to disarm, make extensive territorial concessions, and pay reparations to certain countries that had formed the Entente powers.

Competing and sometimes conflicting goals among the victors resulted in a compromise that left none content; Germany was neither appeased nor conciliated, nor was it considerably weakened. The League of Nations was officially formed because of the Paris Peace Conference, but the U.S. opted not to join.

Council of Four at the WWI Paris Peace Conference (David Lloyd George, Vittorio Orlando, Georges Clemenceau, Woodrow Wilson), May 27, 1919

Impact of WWI

WWI was disastrous for nearly all participants, having wrought unprecedented destruction in Europe and leaving an estimated 9 to 13 million dead. It proved to be the end of the **Empire Age**. By 1920, as borders were reestablished according to armistices and treaties, the maps of Europe and the Middle East became vastly different from those of a mere decade earlier. The **German Empire**, **Ottoman Empire,** and **Austro-Hungarian Empire** were destroyed. The **British Empire**, though victorious in this war, was witnessing the last of its glory days with the rise of anti-colonial nationalism within its own realm. The only nation to emerge economically stronger than before was the U.S. The global power balance was shifting.

AMENDMENTS & OTHER LEGISLATION

16th Amendment • February 3, 1913

This amendment gave Congress the ability to levy and collect a direct federal income tax from individuals and corporations.

17th Amendment • April 8, 1913

Two senators represent each state in six-year terms. This amendment established the direct election, or election by the people, of senators. Prior to this amendment's ratification, state legislatures elected senators.

Federal Reserve Act • December 23, 1913

Since the early 1870s, the U.S. had experienced a multitude of financial and banking panics, most recently the financial panic of 1907 when the stock market crashed, banks fell, and credit was dashed. The government was unable to curtail the crisis and had to rely on independent bankers like J.P. Morgan to fix the system by contributing capital. As a result, a movement for the creation of a central banking authority emerged. Americans sought an organized entity that could help keep the country's currency elastic by adjusting the money supply while maintaining a healthy banking system. Democrats in Congress created and passed the Federal Reserve Act. On December 23, 1913, President Woodrow Wilson signed the act, which created a decentralized central bank.

18ᵗʰ Amendment • 1919-1933

The **Temperance** movement, a push to ban the consumption of alcoholic drinks, was active at the turn of the 20ᵗʰ century. This reform movement was tied to other social reforms and moral movements and largely driven by women and churches. It paved the way for the 18ᵗʰ Amendment, which banned the manufacture, transportation, and sale of alcohol and established **Prohibition** nationwide. It went into effect in January of 1920. Prohibition proved to be unsuccessful and was later repealed by the 21ˢᵗ Amendment in 1933.

Authorities pouring beer into the gutters in 1920

Volstead Act • October 28, 1919

Though President Woodrow Wilson attempted to veto Prohibition, Congress overrode him and passed the Volstead Act (also known as the National Prohibition Act). It was named after the Republican representative who championed it, Andrew J. Volstead. This act outlined the details of the nationwide ban on alcohol production, sale, and consumption. It was passed in order to guarantee that the 18ᵗʰ Amendment could be enforced.

CIVIL RIGHTS

===

Marcus Garvey • 1887-1940

During this year, Garvey, inspired by Booker T. Washington's autobiography, founded the **Universal Negro Improvement Association** (UNIA) in his birth country, Jamaica, with Amy Ashwood. Branches of this organization could be found all over the United States, the Caribbean, Central America, Canada, and Africa by 1920. Garvey also founded a **"Back to Africa"** movement that was the forerunner of "Black Nationalism."

Great Migration • c. 1915-1960s

During WWI, African Americans who primarily lived in rural, southern regions of the U.S. began to move westward and to urban, northern areas to seek employment in the wartime industries. An estimated six million African Americans migrated to these regions from the oppression of the south, resulting in a significant demographic shift.

Red Summer • 1919

WWI resulted in a mass migration of African Americans from the South to the North to participate in the war effort. After the war, however, African Americans received the same treatment they had before the war had begun. As a result, violence erupted across the nation. Both northern and southern cities in the United States experienced racial turmoil and rioting during this period. Washington, D.C., Chicago, Illinois, and Elaine, Arkansas, experienced some of the most violent events. Throughout the nation, hundreds were killed, thousands injured, and many more displaced. This differed from previous racial riots in that African Americans had developed a new sense of confidence in politics, society, and art; they fought back. President Woodrow Wilson remained inactive.

BIG BUSINESS & LABOR

Triangle Shirtwaist Factory, 1911
New York World

Triangle Shirtwaist Fire
March 25, 1911

The Triangle Shirtwaist Factory, an industrial sweatshop located in New York City, was engulfed in flames. One hundred and forty-six workers, most of whom were female, teenage European immigrants, were unable to escape due to locked exits and poor safety features and perished in the fire. This horrific and preventable tragedy brought attention to deplorable sweatshop conditions in industrial factories and fueled the flames of the labor movement and movements to improve working conditions for women and immigrants.

Standard Oil Co. of New Jersey v. United States
May 15, 1911

This court case challenged the monopoly of industrialist **John D. Rockefeller**, who exercised enormous power over the United States oil industry through his company, Standard Oil. The court declared it to be an unlawful monopoly and, by the provisions of the Sherman Antitrust Act, disassembled the company that had made Rockefeller the richest man in the world, Standard Oil.

Ford's moving assembly line • 1913

Henry Ford of Ford Motor Company made way for mass production of the automobile with the creation of the first moving assembly. Ford employed the concepts of interchangeable parts, continuous flow, division of labor, and reduction of wasted effort to drastically accelerate the manufacturing process and make cars more affordable and accessible for the American public. Other industries incorporated his manufacturing principles into their production.

Clayton Antitrust Act • 1914

At President Woodrow Wilson's urging, Congress passed the Clayton Antitrust Act to reinforce the Sherman Antitrust Act of 1890, a lenient piece of antitrust legislation that had failed to curb the growth of big business and was vague and full of loopholes. The Clayton Antitrust Act clearly defined monopolies and included provisions to prevent price discrimination, exclusive deals, and anticompetitive mergers. It also encouraged the filing of private lawsuits and forbade corporations from preventing their workers from organizing labor unions.

Seattle General Strike of 1919 • February 6, 1919

Trade unionists of Seattle opted to go on strike. In light of the Bolshevik Revolution and WWI, fear and anti-labor stances rose among Americans. The state responded by threatening the striking workers with violence, and their labor leaders were cautious, causing the workers to resume their work and killing the strike. This heightened the **Red Scare**, or general American fear of communist revolution coming to the U.S., and some people became targets by the press and law.

SPORTS & ATHLETES

Jim Thorpe's Olympic victories • 1912

Jim Thorpe (1888-1953) competed in the 1912 Summer Olympics in Stockholm, Sweden. He was of Native American ancestry, Sac and Fox, and hailed from Oklahoma. Thorpe was an extraordinary athlete and won gold in both the pentathlon and the decathlon. However, his medals were taken from him when it was revealed that he had once been paid to play Minor League baseball and was not an amateur athlete. He went on to play professional baseball and football, alongside acting in many Hollywood films.

Black Sox Scandal • October 1919

The Chicago White Sox, like many other baseball teams of the period, were not paid much. This led them to engage in gambling and other gambits to earn money. A group of White Sox players made a deal to throw the World Series game in return for a profit. As a result, their opponents, the Cincinnati Reds, won the title, and the involved player's careers were shattered.

Jack Dempsey • 1895-1983

William "Jack" Dempsey was born in Manassa, Colorado, and known as "the Manassa Mauler." He began boxing in 1914 and built an impressive career. From 1919 to 1926, Dempsey reigned as the world's heavyweight boxing champion. He was characterized as tough, ruthless, quick, and always on the offensive. Dempsey finally lost his title to Gene Tunney. After the match, Dempsey told his wife, "Honey, I forgot to duck." In 1927, the two fighters met again in a match called the **Battle of the Long Count**. Tunney won. Dempsey was one of the most influential American sports icons of the twenties, or the golden age of sports.

LITERATURE & JOURNALISM

Establishment of the Pulitzer Prize • 1917

Joseph Pulitzer, a 19th century newspaper publisher, used journalism to combat government corruption and changed the way newspapers of the day reported events. The Pulitzer Prizes were established by a provision he included in his will. These prestigious awards are bestowed for skillful journalism and other categories.

Edgar Rice Burroughs • 1875-1950

Burroughs, an author and fan of pulp fiction, decided to pen his own series. Thus Tarzan, an English nobleman's son lost and raised by apes in the African wilderness, was born. After first appearing in installments in magazines, *Tarzan of the Apes* was published in 1912 and followed by 24 other Tarzan novels. Burroughs established a corporation in 1923 and began to publish his works without aid of a middleman. Tarzan was not only a literary sensation, but also a cinematic one and has been played by many actors in various films and television shows.

Carl Sandburg • 1878-1967

Sandburg, the son of Swedish immigrants, was an author, poet, journalist folklorist, and historian. He was politically active and wrote about the conditions experienced by American laborers. One of his first major works was *Cornhuskers* (1918), for which he won the Poetry Society of America prize. He also wrote a two-volume biography called *Abraham Lincoln: The Prairie Years* (1926) and a four-volume follow-up called *Abraham Lincoln: The War Years* (1939) which won him a Pulitzer Prize in History. In 1951, he took home a second Pulitzer Prize for his *Complete Poems*.

ART & CINEMA

Indiana Glass Works Boys by Lewis Hine, 1908

Lewis Hine • 1874-1940

Lewis Hine was an American sociological photographer. He proved that the medium could be used as an instrument for change when his photographs of the condition of sweatshops, coal mines, farms, and textile mills helped the National Child Labor Committee (NCLC) incense the public and government to pass child labor laws. Hine was a pioneer of the concept of photography as a documentary tool and catalyst for change.

D.W. Griffith • 1875-1948

Griffith was an early American filmmaker who is often credited with turning film into an art form by pioneering new innovations, including camera angles, lighting, and editing techniques. Though he produced many films, perhaps his most famous was ***Birth of a Nation*** (1915). Based on Thomas Dixon's novel *The Clansman*, it is an innovative but highly controversial silent film about two families during the Civil War and Reconstruction. The film presents freed slaves in the South and Reconstruction in a bad light (Griffith hailed from the South, and his father had fought for the Confederacy). It is racist propaganda but was presented as historical fact at the time. It made an enormous profit and is often hailed as Hollywood's first "blockbuster." Despite its controversial history, this film was one of the first to introduce innovative camera techniques like close-ups and is shown in film classes today. It was also the first film screened in the White House (this screening occurred during Woodrow Wilson's presidency).

SIGNIFICANT EVENTS

Boy Scouts established • February 8, 1910

On this day, the Boy Scouts of America was founded. The Girl Scouts (originally called the American Girl Guides) was established on March 12, 1912 by Juliette Gordon Low.

RMS *Titanic,* 1912

RMS *Titanic* • 1909-1912

During the first half of the 20th century, shipping lines were very competitive. The White Star Line was in a steamship supremacy rivalry with Cunard, a company that was, ironically enough, the creator of another doomed ship — the *Lusitania*. White Star Line created a ship of gigantic proportions, the *Titanic*. On its first voyage, the ship hit an iceberg and sunk, despite claims of being "unsinkable." More than 1,500 passengers and crewmen lost their lives. The site of the shipwreck was rediscovered off the coast of Newfoundland in 1985. The events of this ill-fated voyage are the setting of a 1996 award-winning fictional film, *Titanic*, which stars Leonardo DiCaprio and Kate Winslett.

South Pole exploration • December 14, 1911

A Norwegian expedition led by **Roald Amundsen** became the first to reach the South Pole. Amundson had beaten his British rival, Robert Falcon Scott, whose party reached the destination a month later, then perished on their return. Interestingly enough, Amundson had embarked on this South Pole expedition after receiving news that he had been beaten to the North Pole by American Robert Peary.

58

New states enter the Union

On January 6, 1912, New Mexico became the 47th state to enter the Union. It was followed by Arizona on February 14, 1912.

Rocky Mountain National Park established January 26, 1915

The land that now makes up this national park was bought by the U.S. as part of the Louisiana Purchase in 1803. A naturalist named Enos Mills campaigned for the area to be named a state park during the U.S. national conservation and preservation movement. With President Woodrow Wilson's signature on the Rocky Mountain National Park Act, it officially became the U.S.' tenth national park in 1915.

Rocky Mountain National Park - National Park Service

Pancho Villa - Library of Congress

Pancho Villa raids 1916

In 1916, a Mexican revolutionary named Pancho Villa (1878-1923) led two raids that left more than 30 Americans dead. Villa led these raids in retaliation against President Wilson's support for his rival, Mexican president Venustiano Carranza. Wilson, who supported Carranza's shift toward democracy, sent General John Pershing on an unsuccessful hunt to capture Villa.

Villa was born Doroteo Arango but changed his name after an altercation with a man who was harassing one of his sisters turned fatal. He began a life as a bandit on the run. During the Mexican Revolution, he became a revolutionary leader and helped Francisco Madero depose dictator Porfirio Díaz. He later created an army to rebel against Victoriano Huerta, a dictator who took power in a coup. Villa controlled much of the military forces in Northern Mexico during this period of time. Interestingly enough, he signed a contract to film some of his battles with Hollywood's Mutual Film Company in 1913. Villa also worked with President Wilson and Emiliano Zapata to depose Carranza. This cooperation, however, was brief, and Wilson ceased to back Villa. This led to Villa's 1916 kidnapping and murder of 18 Americans and then to his raids in March of 1916 that left an additional 19 Americans from Columbus, New Mexico, dead. As a result, General John Pershing was sent to capture him by Wilson but his efforts proved unsuccessful.

U.S. Virgin Islands • March 31, 1917

The U.S. bought an island chain which included St. Thomas, St. Croix, and St. John from Denmark for $25 million dollars and took control on this date. They are located between the Caribbean Sea and Atlantic Ocean. Today, these islands host a healthy tourist industry.

Schenck v. United States • January-March 1919

During WWI, many soldiers were drafted. Charles Schenck began sending mailers to draftees urging them not to cooperate. He claimed the draft was a capitalist driven project and suggested that the draftees attempt to repeal the Conscription Act. Schenck was accused of encouraging insubordination in the military and obstructing recruitment. He was charged with conspiracy to violate the Espionage Act, a law restricting American civil liberties in the name of eliminating wartime infiltration by the Central Powers. Schenck's circulars compared conscripts to convicts and called upon the 13th Amendment as support for this position. Justice Oliver W. Holmes, Jr. wrote that everything must be considered in context and that what might be tolerable in peacetime could be punishable in times of war. Holmes cited **"clear and present danger"** as something that had to be considered when discussing how much tolerance can be given to the concept of free speech. This was the first case that used "clear and present danger" as a litmus test for rights guaranteed by the 1st Amendment.

Boston Molasses Disaster - Library of Congress

Boston Molasses Disaster January 15, 1919

During this period, molasses was a popular sweetener in the U.S. A molasses tank broke and loosed two million gallons of the substance into the streets of Boston, Massachusetts, killing 21 people, injuring 150 more, and causing significant destruction.

NOTABLES & TRIVIA

FORD CONTROVERSY

Henry Ford of Ford Motor Company was one of the most renowned industrialists of the period. However, public opinion was swayed from his favor by the media. Though the media was all for it, Ford was not on board with the idea of war with Mexico in 1916. Thus, the *Chicago Tribune* waged war on Ford's public image, going as far as calling him an anarchist. Ford was infuriated and filed a lawsuit against the newspaper. The *Tribune* was found guilty in 1919 but only fined six cents.

Universal Pictures,

now known as **Universal Studios**, was founded in 1912 by Carl Laemmle. This motion-picture studio would go on to become a leading producer of 1920s low-budget film serials and 1930s horror films.

Intervention of Fate?

Industrialist J.P. Morgan had a suite reserved on the *Titanic's* ill-fated voyage, but cancelled. Other famous folks who were supposed to be aboard but, for one reason or another, did not set sail with the *Titanic* included Theodore Dreiser, Milton Snavely Hershey, and Alfred Gwynne Vanderbilt.

Pyrex Glass · 1915 - When her earthenware casserole dish cracked while baking, Bessie Littleton asked her husband, a physicist employed at Corning Glass Works, if she could try the glass he was testing at work for railroad lantern and battery jar usage. She successfully confirmed its suitability for baking. Corning then launched the first line of consumer temperature-resistant glass cooking products and dubbed it Pyrex.

In 1912, a man named John Schrank attempted to assassinate Teddy Roosevelt before a campaign speech and, after being shot, Roosevelt gave his speech and said, "It takes more than that to kill a Bull Moose." Roosevelt survived the assassination attempt but did not win the election.

Louis Chevrolet, racer, and William Durant, founder of GM, established **Chevrolet Motor Company** in Detroit in 1911.

ZIP-EE!

Though Elias Howe, inventor of the sewing machine, created a version of the zipper in 1851, he failed to market it. In 1893, Whitcomb Judson marketed a clasp zipper. However, it wasn't until Gideon Sundback joined Whitcomb and Colonel Lewis Walker's Universal Fastener Company that the modern zipper was created in 1913. The new innovation was called the "separable fastener" and patented in 1917.

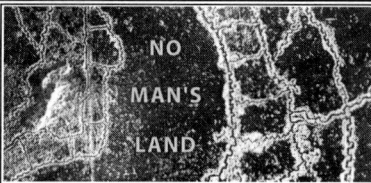

Allied and German trenches were dug in a zigzag pattern deep enough for a soldier to stand and constructed parallel and facing toward each other. A barbed wire fence was thrown up in front of troops in the front lines of the trenches, and the short space between the two enemy's trenches was dubbed "No Man's Land." Conditions in these trenches were horrendous.

Many states gave women the right to vote before suffrage was attained at the national level. In 1913, **Alice Paul** cofounded the Congressional Union and, in 1916, the National Woman's Party. Her strategies to gain suffrage included organizing demonstrations like pickets and hunger strikes. She was arrested and force-fed but ultimately pressured President Wilson to support a suffrage amendment.

Further innovations were developed to combat the stalemate during WWI. One example was the refinement and use of chemical warfare. Germany's usage of chlorine gas in April of 1915 at Ypres was its first successful employment. The Allies followed their lead and began waging chemical warfare. Physically, chemical warfare was not as devastating as other methods due to its reliance on a plethora of factors, but it proved to be a very effective psychological weapon.

✺✺✺ NATIONAL NOTABLES ✺✺✺

American Cancer Society founded, 1913

Prufrock and Other Observations by T. S. Eliot, 1917

Jeanette Rankin became the first American woman to the serve in the House of Representatives, representing the state of Montana, in 1917. She had long fought for suffrage and women's rights and was a steadfast pacifist. Rankin voted against entering both World War I and World War II during her political career.

The **National Hockey League** (NHL) was created in 1917 and was composed of five Canadian teams. In 1924, the Boston Bruins became the first team to represent the U.S. in the league. By 1926, the NHL became the dominant hockey league and possessor of the Stanley Cup, in which Eastern and Western Conference teams duke it out for each annual championship game.

CHAPTER 3

The Roaring Twenties

1920-1929

CONTEXT

The 1920s were a period of economic prosperity in America but also a period of dramatic social and political change. The "Great War" was over, and Americans turned their focus inward and away from Europe, looking to the government for solutions to their problems.

For the first time in American history, the annual census reported that more Americans lived in urban regions than rural ones. At this time, any city with more than 2,000 people was considered urban. New technology and the further decrease in automobile prices increased mobility and improved the lives of the American people. Consumerism was on the rise, and people across the country were listening to the same music and buying the same goods at chain stores.

Prohibition officially began during this decade, but rather than ceasing to drink, Americans found ways to drink outside of the law, and a Prohibition culture developed. Economic prosperity led to the rise of new leisure activities, such as jazz music, dances like the Charleston, the film and Hollywood industry, and the attendance of athletic events, particularly baseball. Most households had access to commercial radio, a spectacular innovation in human communication.

During WWI, women had successfully held jobs that were normally considered male occupations and discovered that holding these jobs was rewarding. Many did not want to return to the pigeonhole life of daughter to wife to mother. Socially, traditional roles of women were also changing dramatically, and they were increasingly adopting "male" habits such as drinking, smoking, and going out to clubs. These changes were most obvious for the middle and upper classes. Despite the glamour of the "Roaring Twenties," many Americans, particularly farmers and African Americans, remained in poverty. Women in these classes often worked in menial labor positions, and marriage at an early age remained common.

That being said, WWI left poverty, ethnic tension, and resentment in Europe and was one reason why there was a surge of immigration to the U.S. The war also contributed to the American people's fear of the influx of immigrants. Russia's revolution in 1917 and the creation of the communist Union of Soviet Socialist Republics (USSR) in 1922 resulted in a "Red Scare," and the racial divide saw the resurrection of hate groups like the Ku Klux Klan (KKK).

This period of spectacular growth and unregulated spending, both by individuals and by the financial organizations of Wall Street, was reaching the tipping point of sustainability, but for now, the war was over and it was time to move forward and try to adapt to a changing consumer-driven society.

PRESIDENTS & ELECTIONS

Election of 1920 • November 2, 1920

WWI was over, nationalist activist Theodore Roosevelt was dead, and global idealist Woodrow Wilson was an invalid. Republican candidate Warren G. Harding of Ohio ran against Democratic candidate James Cox of Ohio. Harding, contrary to Roosevelt's activism and Wilson's idealism, promised the American people a "return to normalcy." Harding won by a landslide, and Calvin Coolidge of Massachusetts served as his vice president. The Election of 1920 was the first election since the passage of the 19th Amendment, and women nationwide voted for the first time!

Warren G. Harding • 1865-1923

Warren G. Harding

Harding was from Ohio and a graduate of Ohio Central College. After graduation, he became a reporter at a newspaper and later purchased and ran his own, the *Marion Star*. His time in politics began in 1898, when he was elected to the Ohio Senate. After that, he served as the state's lieutenant governor for two years before he was elected to serve in the U.S. Senate. In 1920, Harding was nominated and ran a front-porch campaign from his home as the Republican candidate. He was elected to the presidency. As president, Harding restricted immigration and was in favor of business, reducing taxes, and enacting protective tariffs. Scandals within his administration that were no fault of his own, like the Teapot Dome Scandal, reflected poorly on his presidency.

Teapot Dome Scandal • 1921-1922

During President Warren G. Harding's administration, **Albert Bacon Fall**, the U.S. secretary of the interior, leased federal oil reserves and collected a profit beneath the table. Fall leased the Teapot Dome reserves to Mammoth Oil Company's Harry F. Sinclair and the Elk Hills and Buena Vista Hills reserves to the Pan American Petroleum Company's Edward L. Doheny. As Harding had shifted the supervision of the oil reserves from the Navy to the Department of the Interior, the stress of the investigation and subsequent Supreme Court order that Harding's decision was illegal impacted his health and political career.

President Warren G. Harding's death • August 2, 1923

President Harding suffered a fatal stroke, and Vice President Calvin Coolidge ascended to the presidency on August 2, 1923. Coolidge was sworn into office by his father, a notary public.

Calvin Coolidge • 1872-1933

Calvin Coolidge

Coolidge, a man of few words who was also known as "Silent Cal," was born in Vermont and a graduate of Amherst College. He established a career in law and politics and served as the governor of Massachusetts before becoming Harding's vice president and his abrupt ascension to the presidency in 1923. As president, he was a minimalist who maintained the status quo, believing the best government to be the least government. However, as the nation appeared to be in a period of prosperity, he was very popular with the American people and was reelected in 1924. Electing to not run for president again, Coolidge left the Oval Office in 1928, a year before the stock market crashed.

Election of 1924 • November 4, 1924

Coolidge, the vice president who had stepped in to complete the last year of Harding's presidential term after his death, received the Republican nomination and ran with the slogan "Keep Cool with Coolidge." He defeated Democratic candidate John W. Davis and Progressive candidate Robert M. La Follette.

Election of 1928 • November 6, 1928

President Calvin Coolidge did not run for re-election. Republican presidential candidate Herbert Hoover soundly defeated Democratic candidate Alfred Smith, winning both the popular and electoral vote. Charles Curtis served as his vice president. Hoover became the first president who had been born west of the Mississippi.

Herbert Hoover

Herbert Hoover • 1874-1964

Hoover was born to a Quaker family in Iowa and orphaned at a young age. He was raised by his uncle. Hoover was a member of Stanford University's first class and graduated in 1895 with a degree in geology. After graduation, he became a mining engineer and worked his way to becoming a multimillionaire. Interestingly enough, he was working in China when the Boxer Rebellion erupted. When WWI began in Europe, he became involved in humanitarian work, and when the U.S. joined as well, he took the helm of the Food Administration at President Woodrow Wilson's request. He later served as the secretary of commerce for both President Harding and President Coolidge. "The Great Humanitarian" was elected to the presidency in the Election of 1928. His term began in 1929, the year that the stock market crashed and the Great Depression began. Hoover was a progressive Republican and pursued federal intervention. While he did not push the same scale of federal government intervention as FDR, he did set the stage. The U.S. sunk deeper into the Depression, and Hoover was perceived as indifferent to the American people's plight. His bid for reelection in 1932 was a failure, and Franklin D. Roosevelt ascended to the presidency.

PROHIBITION

Prohibition begins • January 1920

Prohibition went into effect, and making, selling, or transporting liquor became illegal. It was unpopular and difficult to enforce. As a result, the 18th Amendment was recalled by the 21st Amendment in 1933. While Prohibition proved unsuccessful, it did, however, jump-start the "Jazz Age" and had a great impact on American culture.

Speakeasies & bootlegging

Though alcohol was illegal, the American people did not cease to drink. As a matter of fact, Prohibition encouraged people nationwide to find creative ways to bypass the law, such as the development of speakeasies and bootlegging.

Bootlegger Charlie Birger (seated, car roof center) & his gang, 1927
Kentucky Historical Society

Speakeasies were illegal bars that served liquor during this era. Bootleggers smuggled illicit alcohol to meet the underground consumer's needs. Alcohol consumption was by no means extinguished. Activities like bootlegging helped to establish organized crime in the nation that outlasted Prohibition itself, such as the Mafia.

WOMEN'S RIGHTS

Women's suffrage movement • c. 1848-1920

The *Declaration of Sentiments* was drafted for the Seneca Falls Convention, which was organized by reformers like Elizabeth Cady Stanton and Lucretia Mott, in 1848. This document declared the genders to be equal and demanded equal rights. The movement continued during the 1850s but was interrupted by the eruption of the Civil War (1861-1865). After the war's conclusion, the 14th and 15th Amendments were passed. In 1870, black men were given citizenship and enfranchised by the 15th Amendment (in theory though not in practice). Groups like the **National American Woman Suffrage Association** were formed, and the suffragist movement remained active, bolstered by the newfound skills and independence women experienced during WWI. Women would not see the same enfranchisement until 1920.

Suffragettes Rose Cumming &
Edith Griffith, c. 1915
Library of Congress

19th Amendment • 1919-1920

After WWI, the almost century-long campaign for women's suffrage was rewarded with the passage of the 19th Amendment; women were enfranchised at the national level, though many had already been granted the right to vote by their respective states. It is important to note that although this enfranchisement was legally extended to African-American women, southern African-American women were often prevented from voting by state laws and other practices. The enfranchisement of southern African-American women would not be realized until the 1960s Civil Rights Movement came into play.

Joan Crawford in flapper attire, 1927
Library of Congress

Flappers • c. 1920s

This was a reference to women of the 1920s who wore dresses with short skirts and high heels, applied cosmetics, bobbed their hair, and were active in urban nightlife. Many went to jazz and vaudeville performances and speakeasies. In August 1920, women had won the right to vote, and they began to challenge accepted social standards. Unlike most generations of women before them, many flappers had jobs. They were representative of the liberal period of the Roaring Twenties and considered somewhat brash. Author F. Scott Fitzgerald's wife, Zelda, belonged to this group.

Birth control & Margaret Sanger • 1921

The Comstock Act had long banned the use of contraceptives. Margaret Sanger, a woman who gave up nursing to champion causes like birth control and sex education, challenged this, founding the American Birth Control League. She was arrested multiple times. In her later years, she sought someone who could develop a birth control pill and was successful. Now, a safer and cheaper alternative to outdated contraception methods could be provided to the masses. Supreme Court case *Griswold v. Connecticut* (1965) later determined that contraceptives were legal by the provisions of the Constitution.

Equal Rights Amendment (ERA) first introduced • 1923

This sought the constitutional guarantee of equal rights for American women and was written by women's rights activist **Alice Paul**. It was reintroduced in each session of Congress for 50 years.

First woman governor • 1924

Nellie Tayloe Ross
Library of Congress

Wyoming elected the first female governor in U.S. history, Nellie Tayloe Ross, to replace her husband who had died while in office. She was Wyoming's 14th governor and served from 1925 to 1927. Texas was soon to follow with its own female governor, Miriam "Ma" Ferguson, also succeeding her husband.

RED SCARE & IMMIGRATION

Palmer Raids • 1919-1920

These raids, perpetrated by Attorney General **Mitchell Palmer**, were the product of unrest stemming from WWI. The armistice had not ended the United States' internal problems like unemployment, violent strikes, and race riots. Palmer introduced the specter of the "Red Menace" and, in turn, the **Red Scare**. During this period, the government arrested those believed to be members of leftist groups and radicals.

American Civil Liberties Union (ACLU)
January 19, 1920

In light of perceived post-WWI civil liberties abuses like the "Palmer Raids," this union was established. The ACLU was involved in the Scopes Trial, which addressed the teaching of evolution in schools. The ACLU still exists today. Its stated purpose is to defend the people's rights as granted by the Constitution.

Sacco-Vanzetti Trial • 1921

At the Red Scare's height, two Italian-Americans named Nicola Sacco and Bartolomeo Vanzetti were accused of murder and the armed robbery of a shoe factory in 1920. As they were both anarchists with radical political affiliations, they were convicted and executed despite the fact that much of the "evidence" brought against them was disproven. Leftist parties around the globe donated millions to the two men's defense.

Immigration Act of 1924

Due to security concerns during WWI, the first seriously restrictive law of this type was passed in 1917; it barred most Asians and required the passage of a literacy test. When it was decided that this was insufficient, the 1924 act was passed and placed quotas on immigrants from particular countries. It reflected fears of foreign influence that persisted in the post-war era. No immigration from Asia would be permitted, but the law did not place quotas on immigration from within the Americas. This legislation was also called the Johnson-Reed Act and was signed by President Calvin Coolidge.

COURT CASES

Leopold and Loeb murder trial • 1924

A 14-year-old boy from a distinguished Chicago family named Bobby Franks was kidnapped and murdered. Two privileged and intelligent youths, 18-year-old Richard Loeb and 19-year-old Nathan Leopold, had murdered their neighbor in an attempt to commit the "perfect crime." Loeb and Leopold were represented by Clarence Darrow. The two pleaded "guilty" and avoided trial by jury. Darrow, a skilled orator, fought the death penalty. Judge John R. Caverly delivered a life sentence.

Scopes Trial • 1925

By the provisions of the Butler Act passed in Tennessee in 1925, public and collegiate educators could not teach the **theory of evolution**. The theory, pioneered by Charles Darwin, collided with the beliefs of creationists. The ACLU provided funding for John T. Scopes, a Tennessee science teacher, to challenge the law in court. Scopes taught evolution in class and was taken to court. Scopes' attorney was Clarence Darrow, and the prosecutor for the state was former presidential candidate William Jennings Bryan.

Scopes was convicted and fined $100 (approximately $1,300 in today's world). Darrow appealed the conviction, and it was heard by the U.S. Supreme Court, which overturned the guilty verdict. This case is also known as *State of Tennessee v. John Thomas Scopes* or the "Monkey Trial." It was the first trial broadcasted to the public by national radio. The Butler Act was not repealed until 1967.

Clarence Darrow - Library of Congress

Clarence Darrow
1857-1938

Darrow was a famous American trial attorney. While he was originally a corporate lawyer, he later became famous labor and criminal lawyer. During his career, he represented strikers, labor leaders, anarchists, and others who were deemed radical leftists. Two of his highest profile cases were the Leopold and Loeb murder trial and the Scopes Trial, where he defended science and the theory of evolution.

William Jennings Bryan • 1860-1925

Also called the "Great Commoner," Bryan was a member of the Democratic Party. He represented Nebraska in the House of Representatives from 1891 to 1895, ran for the presidency a grand total of three times during his political career but was never victorious, and served as secretary of state under Woodrow Wilson from 1913 to 1915. After resigning his position as secretary of state, he opposed Scopes' lawyer, Clarence Darrow, in the Scopes Trial. Though Bryan won the case, this outcome was successfully appealed. Five days after the trial's close, a worn-out Bryan passed away.

William Jennings Bryan - Library of Congress

TECHNOLOGIES & DISCOVERIES

Washing machine refined

Though invented decades earlier, the newer washing machines of the 1920s were a vast improvement. For one, they did not shred the clothes they cleaned. They were cheaper and could wash larger loads of clothing. This eased the workload of the typical homemaker.

Discovery of King Tutankhamun's tomb • 1922

Howard Carver with the sarcophagus of King Tutankhamun
The New York Times

The burial place of this ancient Egyptian pharaoh, popularly known as "King Tut," was revealed by British Egyptologist **Howard Carter** and the man who had funded the excavation, George Herbert. While many Egyptian mummies had been discovered, this one was hailed as a particularly magnificent discovery due to the fact that his tomb was miraculously undisturbed and full of riches. Tut captivated the globe. Public fascination resulted in what has since been called "Nile Style," and Egyptian themes were integrated into the Art Deco style and permeated art, music, fashion, cinema, furnishings, and much more. This fascination was particularly interesting if you take into account the fact that Tut was a weak teenage pharaoh who was dominated by his advisers; his fame was greater in death than in life.

Model T and the automobile economy • 1924

By 1924, the cost of cars was down to $260, and loans were readily available. Along with the mass production of the automobile came an industry to support it. Service stations sprouted along major roadways, and as people traveled farther, they needed overnight accommodations and a place to eat. Motels and diners soon dotted the highways and byways of the nation.

Frozen food • 1924

In 1924, Clarence Birdseye created a way to quick-freeze foods that did not result in a change of taste or texture so that his family could have fruits and vegetables all year. While living in Labrador, he had observed Inuits in the Arctic preserving fish by freezing them in subzero temperatures. He then perfected an efficient system for freezing and packaging foods. Though initially designed to ensure off-season produce was available all year, frozen food soon became a convenience food.

Charles Lindbergh flight May 20-21, 1927

American aviator Charles Lindbergh (1902-1974) made the first nonstop, solo transatlantic flight in a monoplane called the *Spirit of St. Louis*. Lindbergh, also known as "Lucky Lindy" and the "Lone Eagle," was a renowned conservationist, pacifist, and advocate of the space program.

Charles Lindbergh - Library of Congress

Amelia Earhart flight • June 17-18, 1928

An American aviatrix, Earhart became the first female to fly across the Atlantic in 1928. During this famous flight, she was the passenger of pilots Wilmer Stutz and Louis Gordon. Regardless, the feat earned her much acclaim, and she attempted her own amazing flight feats during the 1930s.

Amelia Earhart - National Library of Ireland

THE GOLDEN AGE OF SPORTS

Professional football • 1920

In 1920, the American Professional Football Association (APFA) was established. It would become the **National Football League** (NFL) we know today in 1922. Jim Thorpe, one of the most famous athletes of the era, was its first president. Can you imagine America without the NFL or Super Bowl Sunday?

Negro National League • 1920

African Americans were not permitted to play on professional baseball teams with white players due to segregation. As a result, this league was established.

Detroit Stars, 1920

First Olympic Winter Games
January 25-February 5, 1924

The first Winter Olympic Games were held in Chamonix, France. There were 16 events and 258 competitors.

Babe Ruth • 1895-1948

Babe Ruth
Library of Congress
George Grantham Bain Collection

George Herman Ruth, Jr. was recruited by Jack Dunn, the Baltimore Orioles' owner, in 1914. His teammates called him "Jack's newest babe," thus lending him his infamous nickname, "Babe." He was also called the "Sultan of Swat" and "Great Bambino." Ruth was traded to the Boston Red Sox, serving as a left-handed pitcher, then to the New York Yankees. It was while batting and playing outfield for the Yankees that he achieved his greatest fame. He became a baseball legend, giving the American people someone to look up to during the Great Depression, and set an astounding 714-homerun record that wouldn't be broken until Hank Aaron came to the scene. Ruth was one of the first five inductees into the National Baseball Hall of Fame.

Lou Gehrig • 1903-1941

Though overshadowed by teammate Babe Ruth to an extent, Gehrig was another of the Yankee's phenomenal hitters and played first base between 1925 and 1939. His career was cut short in 1939 when he was diagnosed with amyotrophic lateral sclerosis (ALS). That same year, he was inducted into the National Baseball Hall of Fame. In 1941, the disease took his life. ALS has since become known as "Lou Gehrig's disease."

ART & ARCHITECTURE

Lincoln Memorial 1922

This monument was constructed between 1914 and 1922 as a tribute to Abraham Lincoln, the 16th president of the United States. Designed by **Daniel Chester French**, it consists of steps leading up to a building supported by Doric columns and features a 19-foot-tall towering marble statue of Lincoln seated on a pedestal. It faces the Reflecting Pool and is located in Washington, D.C.

Lincoln Memorial
Photo by David Bjorgen

Yankee Stadium • 1923

During this period, attending athletic events became an important American leisure activity. In 1920, the Yankees acquired baseball sensation George Hermann "Babe" Ruth. This caused the turnout at Yankee games to skyrocket and their relationship with the Giants, from whom they rented a space to play, to deteriorate. As a result, the Yankee Stadium, located in Bronx, New York, was completed in 1923. It was the first sports arena to be labeled a stadium.

Holland Tunnel • 1927

The Holland Tunnel connects Manhattan, New York, with Jersey City, New Jersey. The tunnel goes under the Hudson River and is now a National Historic Civil and Engineering Landmark. Many of the design and building methods used to create this structure are still used today in the construction of underwater traffic tunnels. Clifford M. Holland, the chief engineer, died before the tunnel was completed.

Sculpture of Mt. Rushmore • 1927-1941

This monument is carved into the face of Mount Rushmore, which is located in South Dakota's **Black Hills**. The team of sculptors that tackled this massive undertaking was led by **Gutzon Borglum**, the son of Danish immigrants. The likenesses of four United States presidents can be found on the mountain's face: George Washington, Thomas Jefferson, Theodore Roosevelt, and Abraham Lincoln. The site is also called the "Shrine of Democracy."

Mount Rushmore - U.S. Federal Government

Art Deco • c. 1920s-1930s

Empire State Building
(an example of Art Deco architecture)
Library of Congress

This art and architecture movement is also known as "style moderne." Art Deco was bold and characterized by simple and clean lines and shapes, mixed materials, and geometric or stylized forms. The first exhibit of this style is often considered to have taken place in Paris at the Exposition Internationale des Arts Décoratifs et Industriels Modernes, though the style did not gain its name until 1968. Art Deco was influenced by popular European art trends at the time, such as the Art Nouveau, Bauhaus, and Cubist movements, among others, and became a major movement in western Europe and the United States during the 1930s. Some Art Deco works were influenced by ancient cultures, such as the Egyptians and Native American groups.

Georgia O'Keeffe • 1887-1986

O'Keeffe was born on a Wisconsin dairy farm and nurtured a desire to become a professional artist from a young age. She attended the Art Institute of Chicago and and University of Virginia. After stints in other careers, O'Keeffe was introduced to alternatives to imitative realism. Her works found their way to Alfred Stieglitz, a photographer and gallery owner who exhibited her artwork. The two later married. O'Keeffe would become one of the America's most famous and prolific Modernist painters. Her focuses included natural forms and New York City architecture. However, she is arguably most famous for works she created while living in New Mexico, including flowers and Southwestern scenes.

LITERATURE

Harlem Renaissance • c. post-WWI-mid-1930s

This movement of expression encompassed African-American literature, art, and intellectualism and essentially resulted in the formation of a new cultural identity. It was centered in Harlem, New York, which became a mecca of sorts for black poets, writers, artists, photographers, musicians, and scholars, and some of its key members were **Langston Hughes**, **Zora Neale Hurston**, Arna Bontemps, and Jean Toomer. While the Renaissance promoted a cultural awakening, it did not break down racial barriers such as Jim Crow laws. Unfortunately, it was some time before the artistry of these men and women was fully appreciated by the world's white communities.

Lost Generation • post-WWI

Gertrude Stein coined the term "Lost Generation" during a conversation with Ernest Hemingway. The term references a disillusioned group of people who reached adulthood during the WWI and the post-WWI period. Many were expatriate American writers who felt distanced from the values of the post-WWI U.S. and traveled to foreign cities. This includes the Parisian group of Hemingway and F. Scott Fitzgerald.

TIME • March 3, 1923

The first issue of *TIME* magazine was printed. Its purpose was to provide readers information about what was going on in the world in a well laid-out and concise fashion. It separated its brief news articles into "departments" like sports, business, and education, and this format was adopted by most other general news magazines. **Henry Luce**, one of its founders, became an influential opinion maker in the U.S. He famously declared in the magazine that the 20th century was the "American Century." *TIME* remains in publication today.

F. Scott Fitzgerald • 1896-1940

Fitzgerald was an American author whose novels captured the spirit of the "Roaring Twenties." He published the novel that would become both his most famous work and an American classic, **The Great Gatsby**, in 1925. This novel did not gain acclaim until after his death. Other important Fitzgerald works include *This Side of Paradise* (1920) and *Tender Is the Night* (1934). His wife Zelda was one of the most famous flappers. Fitzgerald's name at birth was Francis Scott Key Fitzgerald; interestingly enough, he coined the term "Jazz Age" and was a distant relative of Francis Scott Key, the man who penned the "Star-Spangled Banner."

Ernest Hemingway • 1899-1961

Hemingway was an American novelist and author of short stories renowned for his masculine, intense, and succinct writing style. He led an active and adventurous life and served as a reporter before becoming an ambulance driver in World War I. After sustaining an injury, he spent some time recovering. He then resumed his active lifestyle, which led him to Paris and a group of authors who encouraged him to write and publish non-journalistic work. He continued his travels, which included time in Spain, Africa, and Cuba, and went on to publish many works, including *The Sun Also Rises* (1926), *The Old Man and the Sea* (1952), *For Whom the Bell Tolls* (1940), and *A Farewell to Arms* (1929). He won the Nobel Prize for Literature in 1954.

Ernest Hemingway in Milan, Italy, 1918
National Archives

Sinclair Lewis • 1885-1951

Lewis was an American novelist who used his works as mediums to critique society. He took up the mantle of causes related to race and gender, challenging accepted social conditions. In 1930, he won a Nobel Prize for Literature. This was a landmark, as he was the first American to claim that honor. Lewis' most prominent novels include *Main Street* (1920), *Babbitt* (1922), and *Arrowsmith* (1925). Lewis coined the term "Babbit," a word that has come to describe someone who blindly conforms to those around them.

Sinclair Lewis

E.E. Cummings • 1894-1962

Cummings was a Harvard graduate who served in WWI. His work, *The Enormous Room* (1922), is based on his experience during the war. After the war's end, he traveled to Paris and studied art. He gained notoriety as a writer and poet, penning 12 volumes of verse. His poetry gained attention for its unconventional qualities, including unusual punctuation, use of capital letters, and phrasing. Though rumors that he had legally changed his name to be spelled in lower case letters circulated, they prove to be unfounded.

CINEMA

Hollywood

Filmmakers began to flock to Hollywood, an area in Los Angeles, California, at the beginning of the 20th century. During the 1900s, film and motion picture technology advanced by leaps and bounds. The advent of nickelodeons in 1905 and war propaganda screenings during WWI increased film's popularity, and the industry continued to expand. These motion pictures, which predated "talkie" films, had no sound other than the live orchestras that accompanied some productions. At the end of the 1920s, sound was introduced, and Hollywood entered its "Golden Age." *Don Juan* (1926) was the first motion picture accompanied by sound, in this case in the form of a score and sound effects. The first "talkie" film with dialogue was *The Jazz Singer* (1927).

Mickey & Minnie Mouse debut • November 18, 1928

Disney's Mickey and Minnie Mouse made their public premiere in an animated film called *Steamboat Willie*. In 1978, Mickey Mouse became the first cartoon character to earn a star on Hollywood's Walk of Fame.

Walt Disney • 1901-1966

Disney developed an interest and aptitude for art at a young age. After returning from driving ambulances for the Red Cross in Europe during WWI, Disney met Ub Iwerks, and the two opened a studio that created animated advertising shorts and cartoon sketches in 1922. When this business failed, Disney opened a new business with his brother, Roy. This enterprise was successful and became the large entertainment conglomerate we know today. Disney pioneered animated cartoon films and became one of the most famous motion picture and television producers of his time.

Charlie Chaplin • 1889-1977

Charlie Chaplin in *The Kid*, 1921
Photo by James Willis Sayer

Chaplin was born in London to parents who were poor music hall performers, and he began performing himself at the tender age of five. His father deserted the family, and his mother died in 1928. Soon after, Chaplin immigrated to the U.S. and signed an acting deal with Keystone Pictures; the rest is history. Chaplin went on to become arguably the most famous silent film comedian, known for his trademark slapstick humor. He played the part of one character, "**the Little Tramp**," throughout most of his films. The Little Tramp was easily recognizable by his fake moustache, bowler hat, and cane.

Buster Keaton • 1895-1966

Keaton was an actor and, later, filmmaker, who came from a family of vaudeville performers. He was renowned for the use of extreme slapstick (including but not limited to being dropped down stairs and thrown through windows), impeccable timing, and his facial expressions. Some of his famous works include *Sherlock, Jr.* (1924), *The Navigator* (1924), and *The General* (1927).

Greta Garbo • 1905-1990

Garbo worked in a department store in Sweden to help support her family, where she attracted attention and eventually modeled for the company's newspaper advertisements and then an advertising film. She received a scholarship to attend an acting school before meeting director Mauritz Stiller, who kick-started her acting career. She came to the U.S. with Stiller and signed with MGM. Garbo became a Hollywood sensation but was indifferent to stardom, declining to sign autographs or attend film premieres and award ceremonies. Perhaps her best-known film appearance was in *Grand Hotel* (1932), which garnered the Academy Award for Best Picture.

Joan Crawford • c. 1908-1977

A girl from San Antonio, Texas, Crawford made a name for herself dancing and moved to the mecca of the American film industry, Hollywood. She landed roles in films and worked her way to become an A-list Hollywood film star for MGM. She later transferred to their rival, Warner Brothers. Crawford was a glamorous fashion icon of the era, and one of her best-known film appearances was in *Grand Hotel* (1932).

Katharine Hepburn • 1907-2003

Hepburn, an American actress who starred both on Broadway and in films, was born to a wealthy family. Like many of the characters she played, she was characterized as quirky, outspoken, and fiercely independent and possessed a memorable accent. One of her best-known films was *Little Women* (1933).

MUSIC

The Gershwin brothers

George Gershwin (1898-1937) and his older brother Ira (1896-1983) were an American songwriting team that took the theatrical world by storm, creating popular songs, Broadway musicals, and motion pictures during this era. The duo were the children of Russian-Jewish immigrants. George was a brilliant composer, and Ira was a lyricist. Their work is symbolic of the Jazz Age and 1920s and 1930s, and one of their most famous works is the Broadway production *Porgy and Bess*. Though George developed a brain tumor and passed away in 1937, Ira continued their work after his brother's death.

Louis Armstrong • 1901-1971

Louis Armstrong - Library of Congress
Gottlieb Collection

Also called "Satchmo," Armstrong was one of the most famous musicians of the Jazz Age. He hailed from New Orleans, the birthplace of jazz, and his mentor was musician Joe "King" Oliver. He worked his way up and eventually moved to Chicago in 1922 to play in Oliver's Creole Jazz Band. Armstrong became an international star and promoted the rise of jazz music. He is best known for his distinct, gravelly singing voice.

Josephine Baker • 1906-1975

Baker was a dancer and entertainer born in St. Louis, Missouri. She established a career in the U.S. and traveled to Paris in the mid-1920s. Baker became a prominent music hall performer there. She was famous for her flamboyant manner of dress, including her legendary banana ensemble, and was a symbol of the vibrancy of African-American culture during this era. Baker was also known as the "Black Pearl" and "Creole Goddess" and fluent in both English and French.

Duke Ellington • 1899-1974

Edward "Duke" Ellington was a pianist who is often hailed as the best jazz composer and bandleader. "It Don't Mean a Thing if it Ain't Got that Swing" was one of his most popular pieces, and he won more than ten Grammy Awards.

Jelly Roll Morton • 1890-1941

Ferdinand Joseph La Menthe went by the name Jelly Roll Morton. He was a pianist, composer, and bandleader who hailed from New Orleans, the epicenter of the jazz movement. Morton was one of the original ragtime pianists of the era and claimed that he was the creator of jazz. While he did not invent jazz, Morton was key in its development and may have been the first to write his compositions down. "Black Bottom Stomp" and "King Porter Stomp" were some of his most well-known works.

Jimmie Rodgers • 1897-1933

Rodgers, also known as "America's Blue Yodeler" and the "Father of Country Music," was a singer, guitarist, and songwriter who helped to bring about country music and its popularity. He became the first Country Music Hall of Fame inductee in 1961.

SIGNIFICANT NAMES & EVENTS

Macy's Thanksgiving Parade • est. 1924

The original Macy's shop opened in 1858 in New York City, New York. In 1924, the location at Manhattan's Herald Square grew to encompass over one million square feet. To celebrate the opening of the "world's largest store," Macy's organized a parade. It had a nursery rhyme theme, included animals borrowed from the Central Park Zoo, and was a success; thousands of people lined the route. The parade has come to be known for its enormous balloons, the first of which appeared in the 1927 event and was an image of animated character Felix the Cat. Today's route is about two-and-a-half miles long, and the annual festivities are attended by millions and televised to tens of millions more each Thanksgiving morning.

Balto saves Nome • January-February 1925

Nome, Alaska, was in the midst of a dangerous diphtheria epidemic. This could be cured with a serum, but the nearest supply was located almost 1,000 miles away in Anchorage, Alaska. Sled dog teams began the journey there, racing the serum to the town during its time of need. Media coverage brought the saga to the homes of Americans everywhere. Musher Gunner Kaasen and his lead husky, Balto, arrived on February 2. Central Park in New York City features a statue of this canine and, in 1995, Balto was featured in an animated film.

KKK march on Washington • August 8, 1925

Based on its 19th century predecessor, the new KKK was founded around 1915. Just as the group of the same name that preceded this organization had, it practiced racism and violence. The KKK was also anti-Catholic and anti-Semitic. While the old KKK was exclusively southern, this became a nationwide organization. The group reached the height of its power during the 1920s and, at one point, was over three-million-strong. About forty thousand of these members became a national spectacle when they marched on Washington, D.C.'s Pennsylvania Avenue in 1925 in their trademark regalia of white hoods and robes.

Great Mississippi Flood of 1927

Much land had been "reclaimed" from the Mississippi River by a complex levee system. A levee on the river at Mounds Landing failed, and a nightmare began. Astonishingly, there were points during this natural disaster where the Mississippi was over 80 miles wide and over 23,000 square miles were plunged beneath water. Hundreds of thousands were uprooted, and the African-American community of the area was treated to severe injustices, including abuses by those who ran relief operations. President Calvin Coolidge's administration did not come to their aid. Many moved (this was a portion of the African American Great Migration to the northern U.S.) from the area, and Herbert Hoover, who had turned his back on the African-American community, was later elected president. When this occurred, many African Americans switched their vote from the Republican to Democratic Party.

Great Mississippi Flood, 1927 - National Archives

Kellogg-Briand Pact • August 27, 1928

After WWI, there were many efforts to keep another global war from happening. This pact between the U.S and many other nations essentially made war illegal, but proved to be idealistic and impossible to enforce.

League of United Latin American Citizens (LULAC) February 17, 1929

Hispanic Americans, like other ethnic groups, were subject to discrimination and segregation. This organization was founded in Corpus Christi, Texas, and was the first to campaign for Hispanic American civil rights. Many Hispanic people remained in regions the U.S. had annexed from Mexico after the Mexican War.

Wall Street Crash • October 1929

Stock prices were falling. On October 24, Black Thursday, panicked investors traded millions of shares. Attempts to stabilize the market failed, and though it improved briefly, the market continued to fall. On October 29, this culminated in what came to be called Black Tuesday; investors again traded millions of shares, and the stock market crashed. This crash was the result of many factors, including unrestrained speculation on risky assets. The nation began its descent from the Roaring Twenties into the Great Depression.

Saint Valentine's Day Massacre • February 14, 1929

A turf war between Chicago mobsters related to the bootlegging trade culminated in this bloody event. Members of the gang led by infamous mob boss Al "Scarface" Capone killed members of a rival gang led by George "Bugs" Moran. The eventual takedown of Capone was immortalized in the song "The Night Chicago Died" (1974), although events in the song are not entirely accurate.

TRIVIA

Notable Names of the 1920s

**Mae West • Fletcher Henderson • Zora Neale Hurston
Albert Einstein • Langston Hughes • Eugene Debs**

Earle Dickson, a man who worked for Johnson & Johnson, was responsible for inventing the Band-Aid. He made them for his wife, who had a tendency to injure herself. His goal was to invent a bandage that could be easily administered without aid; thus, the adhesive bandage was born.

ENTERTAINMENT
BASKETBALL

In 1926, Abe Saperstein created a basketball team called the Savoy Big Five. By the next year, the team was touring and had changed its name. The **Harlem Globetrotters** were born. The Globetrotters' trademark comedic element was later introduced, and the group has even had its own cartoon TV show.

Comedic legend **Charlie Chaplin** died in 1977. Several months after his death, his coffin was stolen. The grave robbers demanded that his wife, Oona, pay a sizable ransom for its return. The robbers were eventually caught and prosecuted and the coffin reinterred — in a concrete vault.

Where would students be without the beloved **spiral notebook**? Okay, so beloved might be a bit much, but seriously, a collection of blank pages gathered together by a spiral binding was a vast improvement over loose pages. It happened in 1924.

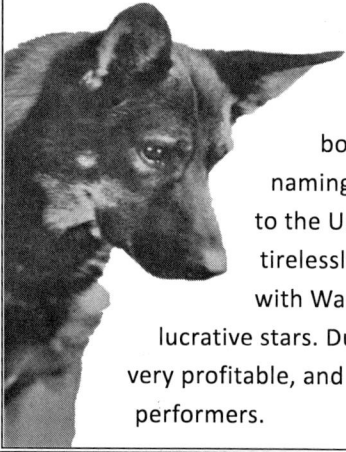

During WWI, an American soldier named Lee Duncan, who was stationed in Eastern France, found a litter of German Shepherd puppies born on a battlefield. Lee kept two of the puppies, naming them Nanette and **Rin Tin Tin**. After returning to the United States with Rin Tin Tin, Duncan worked tirelessly to train him. In the end, Rin Tin Tin won a role with Warner Brothers and became one the studio's most lucrative stars. Duncan's screenplay, *Where the North Begins*, was very profitable, and Rin Tin Tin was one of the studio's highest-paid performers.

TELEVISION

In September of 1927, a 21-year-old American named **Philo Taylor Farnsworth II** successfully demonstrated the ability of his new invention — a primitive form of the television. RCA later bought a license to refine his design and began selling televisions and creating programming to broadcast to viewers. It would not become a major form of mass media until a few decades later, however.

SILVER SCREEN SPY

Actress Greta Garbo is rumored to have worked for the British intelligence agency MI6 during WWII and served as a spy. That being said, a British double-agent nicknamed "Garbo" operated in Europe during this time. His real name was Juan Pujol Garcia.

In 1921, a restaurant chain in Texas called the Pig Stand opened the **"drive-in" restaurant**. Hungry customers would park in a parking lot where their orders were taken and delivered on trays by carhops. Its speed and efficiency was appealing to American consumers.

GUM!

Gum, of some sort, has been chewed since the times of the ancient Greeks. Native Americans chewed spruce sap, and later the colonists added beeswax. The Mayans chewed chicle, the sap of the sapodilla tree. However, the invention of sweet, pink bubble-producing gum did not happen until 1928 when Walter Diemer perfected a recipe by Frank H. Fleer to create **Dubble Bubble**.

One of the most popular dances of this era was the **Charleston**, but the cake walk and the flea hop were also popular.

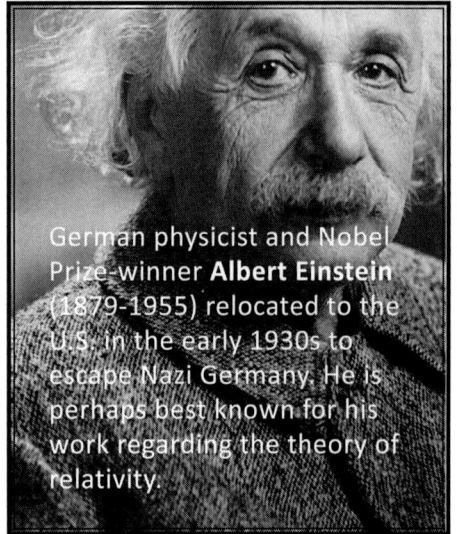

German physicist and Nobel Prize-winner **Albert Einstein** (1879-1955) relocated to the U.S. in the early 1930s to escape Nazi Germany. He is perhaps best known for his work regarding the theory of relativity.

Georgia O'Keeffe was diagnosed with macular degeneration, a disease which results in a deterioration of eyesight. As a result, she painted her final oil painting without assistance in the early 70s. Rather than retiring from art, O'Keeffe hired people to help her create the art she envisioned. The 90-year-old artist once said, "I can see what I want to paint. The thing that makes you want to create is still there."

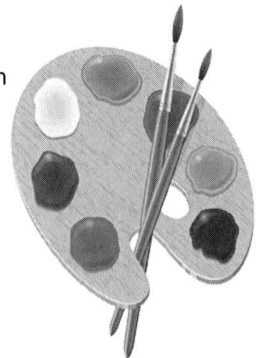

CHAPTER 4
The Great Depression
1930-1939

CONTEXT

In October of 1929, the stock market crashed. This caused a panic which dominoed, developing into a nationwide depression with rampant inflation and unemployment. Roughly 25 percent of all able-bodied workers were unemployed. President Herbert Hoover and his administration failed to curb the economic disaster. It eventually impacted Europe and the rest of the globe. In 1932, Democratic candidate Franklin D. Roosevelt won the presidential election. Roosevelt championed "a **New Deal** for the American people" which included federal programs and institutions that aided the nation's recovery.

The stock market crash was exacerbated by the **Dust Bowl**, which devastated American agriculture. During the 1930s, the Great Plains region, which encompasses portions of Texas, Oklahoma, Kansas, Colorado, and New Mexico, experienced a serious drought. This region's lands had been exploited throughout the 19th and early 20th centuries, and poor farming practices set the stage for this disaster. New Deal agencies were created in order to help farmers repair damage to the land.

Prohibition had proven to be unenforceable and caused an increase in crime. As a result, it was ended by the **21st Amendment** in 1933.

The reality for many small farmers and 'Mom and Pop' shop owners throughout the South and West was that the failure of their small farms and businesses had a greater impact on other people, collectively, than the stock market crash had on them. A song written by Bob McDill and made famous by the country group Alabama in 1989 sums up the times, for many, quite nicely:

"Well somebody told us Wall Street fell
But we were so poor that we couldn't tell
Cotton was short and the weeds were tall
But Mr. Roosevelt's a gonna save us all

Well, momma got sick and daddy got down
The county got the farm and they moved to town
Pappa got a job with the TVA
He bought a washing machine and then a Chevrolet"

California became a popular destination, and soon the state saw an influx that eventually reached almost 400,000 people. For the poor farmer, life remained harsh. California was not the Eden they envisioned when they left their homes in the Midwest and South. Farm unions began supporting the hiring of white "**Okies,**" who became a subculture within California, rather than the migrant Mexican workers that had traditionally worked in the Southern California fields. Deportations occurred, and racial tensions increased and have never truly recovered. Filipinos who had immigrated to the U.S. were also targeted as a threat to American workers, which resulted in the **Filipino Repatriation Act** in 1935.

The Depression would not see its end until WWII, when wartime industry helped the U.S. recover.

PRESIDENTS & ELECTIONS

Election of 1932 • November 8, 1932

With two exceptions, the presidential office had been occupied by Republican heads of state since the opening of the Civil War. The incumbent president, Republican Herbert Hoover, was defeated by Democratic candidate Franklin Delano Roosevelt. Due in part to the Great Depression, this election signaled a shift in the views of the American public.

Franklin D. Roosevelt (FDR) • 1882-1945

Franklin D. Roosevelt

FDR was born in New York and a graduate of Harvard University who passed the bar exam after studying at Columbia Law School. His family was affluent, and he was a fifth cousin of Theodore Roosevelt, whose niece, Eleanor, he married. After briefly practicing corporate law, he began a career in politics. While Teddy, his idol, was a member of the Republican Party, FDR belonged to the Democratic Party. He was elected to the New York State Senate in 1910 and later appointed assistant secretary of the Navy by President Wilson. In 1920, he was nominated to run as the vice presidential Democratic candidate alongside James Cox. FDR was diagnosed with polio in 1921 and took a break from politics. In 1928, he was elected the governor of New York. He ran as the Democratic presidential nominee in the Election of

1932 and defeated incumbent Herbert Hoover to become the 32nd president of the U.S. (1933-1945). He would be elected to the office an unprecedented four times. FDR held this office during two of the nation's greatest trials, the Great Depression and WWII. His New Deal reforms expanded the powers of the federal government.

Fireside chats • 1933-1944

Roughly 90 percent of Americans owned a radio during this era. FDR took advantage of this fact, using radio as a way to address the American public, assuage their fears, and boost morale during this harsh period of American history, which included both the Great Depression and WWII. The 30 informal broadcasts he gave were called "fireside chats," and the first was given in March 1933.

Eleanor Roosevelt • 1884-1962

Eleanor Roosevelt

Eleanor Roosevelt, wife of Franklin D. Roosevelt, served not only as First Lady, but also as a humanitarian and diplomat. When FDR was incapacitated by polio, Eleanor took on an active role in Democratic politics, traveling and reporting the condition of the nation to him. She was very involved in charity and advocated for the rights of women, minorities, and others who were disadvantaged. Though her husband died in 1945, her involvement in politics did not end there. She was involved in many organizations and served as a U.S. delegate to the U.N. from about 1946 to 1953.

Gallup polls • 1935

The American Institute of Public Opinion was established by Dr. George Gallup in 1935. This organization independently measured public opinion and has since become known as the Gallup Poll organization. To avoid skewed results, Gallup polls are not sponsored or paid for by special-interest groups.

Election of 1936 • November 3, 1936

President Franklin D. Roosevelt was popular, but New Deal policies like the Social Security Act and Works Progress Administration had alienated some members of the U.S population. In the general election, FDR ran against Republican candidate Alf Landon and, with the support of farmers, laborers, and the poor, was reelected.

LEGISLATION

New Deal • 1933

The New Deal refers to domestic liberal legislation passed during FDR's administration to help the ailing economy and the American people. Reform included changes in the arenas of industry, agriculture, finance, labor, housing, and waterpower. This liberal legislation increased the government's scope, moving from the traditional "laissez-faire" approach to government regulation, and ultimately altered the federal government's role. The term "New Deal" can be traced back to FDR's 1932 presidential nomination acceptance speech. FDR's initial three months in office were called the **Hundred Days**, and it was during this time frame that the majority of the New Deal was passed. Though much of this legislation was widely popular, proponents of some businesses and states' rights and small government advocates opposed it.

Civilian Conservation Corps (CCC) • 1933-1942

This public works project was one of the first of many New Deal programs. Its ultimate goals were to give young or unemployed men work while molding them into quality citizens through outdoor labor and to encourage environmental conservation. Alongside other environmental conservation efforts, members of the CCC worked to conserve soil, reforest the land, and plant millions of trees. Almost three million young men were a part of this program.

Tennessee Valley Authority Act • May 18, 1933

This act was signed by FDR and created a government agency called the Tennessee Valley Authority (TVA). It worked to improve the condition of the

Tennessee River, which was prone to flooding and difficult to travel due to the shallow Muscle Shoals. It also worked to improve the lives of the people residing in the Tennessee Valley, many of whom were poor and did not have electricity. The TVA provided aid to businessmen and farmers in the area, encouraging industrial development, improving soil quality, and reforesting the area. It was a grand success, and the TVA remains the nation's largest public power company.

21st Amendment • December 5, 1933

Prohibition was largely ignored by the American public, resulting in a thriving bootlegging industry and speakeasies. Its unpopularity and the difficulty of enforcing it led to the 21st Amendment, which repealed the 18th Amendment and ended Prohibition. Beer with a low alcohol percentage was legalized. In response, the Anheuser-Busch brewing company delivered some of their beer directly to the White House and President Franklin D. Roosevelt, who had pledged to end Prohibition, by their signature Clydesdale horses. Americans were enthusiastic about the ban's lift (and the public loved Anheuser-Busch's publicity stunt).

Indian Reorganization Act • June 18, 1934

By this period, many recognized that the United States' Native American policies had caused poverty within Native communities. FDR's administration altered U.S. policy for Native American groups with the passage of this act, also known as the "Wheeler-Howard Act." Its goal was to help Native groups develop economically and become more autonomous, while assuring them more civil rights. Many groups created constitutions, rather than governing by their traditional customs. About 181 tribes voted to adopt it, while 77 did not, fearing the federal government's control.

(Cont. from p. 110) John Collier, Commissioner of Indian Affairs, meets with
with South Dakota Blackfoot chiefs, 1934

Social Security Act (SSA) • August 14, 1935

This act was a piece of Franklin D. Roosevelt's New Deal legislation. In
essence, it created a federal system to provide for the elderly, unemployed
workers, those who suffered from industrial accidents, mothers and children,
the blind, and those who were physically challenged.

Works Progress Administration (WPA) • 1935-1943

FDR established the WPA by way of an executive order. This is one of the
most famous facets of FDR's New Deal. It was a relief program led by Harry
Hopkins and aimed to give the unemployed a job rather than handing
out money. Those employed by the WPA constructed bridges and roads,
alongside public buildings, parks, and airports and other buildings. It also
found ways to help professionals in the creative arts by sponsoring plays, art
projects, and publications.

Historic Sites Act • August 21, 1935

This legislation provided for the preservation of "historic sites, buildings, and objects of national significance for the inspiration and benefit of the people of the United States."

Court-Packing Plan • February 5, 1937

FDR announced that he planned to enlarge the Supreme Court. Many perceived this as a plan to "pack" the court, or appoint judges that would support his legislation. The Republican-dominated Supreme Court had struck down some important New Deal policies over the previous two years, condemning them as examples of federal and executive overreach. Before this bill could be voted on, two of the Supreme Court's justices began to vote liberally, supporting FDR's legislation, and made court-packing unnecessary.

This was one of the most unpopular things that FDR did during his presidency and started extensive infighting within the Democratic Party. It also caused a major showdown in future New Deal programs.

National minimum wage set • June 1938

The Fair Labor Standards Act set a minimum wage of 25 cents an hour, banned employing minors in most scenarios, and established time and a half for overtime, among other things. Its goal was to improve labor conditions. The act, also called the Wages and Hours Act, was sponsored by a senator from New York, Robert F. Wagner.

CRIME WAVE

J. Edgar Hoover & the FBI

As Prohibition had inspired a growth in crime and gangs, the Great Depression created hard times that inspired a crime wave. The Federal Bureau of Investigation (FBI) combatted the problem with J. Edgar Hoover at its helm. They monitored criminals like Al Capone, alongside the Ku Klux Klan and white supremacists. The American public was fascinated by both the war on crime and the outlaws and desperadoes involved.

Bonnie Parker & Clyde Barrow
Library of Congress

Bonnie & Clyde

Clyde Barrow and Bonnie Parker met in Texas and began one of the most infamous romances and criminal partnerships in American history. Bonnie joined Clyde in his career of thievery and life on the run. The two are most famous for a two-year-long deadly bank and store robbing spree that spanned five states. This spree and their criminal careers were terminated in 1934, when the two were shot and killed by police in Louisiana. Interestingly enough, though the two were treacherous and murderous outlaws, they were romanticized by the American public and have become legends. In 1967, Bonnie was played by Faye Dunaway and Clyde by Warren Beatty in a successful film.

John Dillinger • c. 1903-1934

John Dillinger, also known as "Jackrabbit" and "Public Enemy No. 1," was a violent gangster and bank robber who became a top news headline during the 1930s. He rampaged through the Midwestern region of the United States committing armed bank robberies with his gang of criminal counterparts between 1933 and July 1934. Dillinger was shot and killed at Biograph Theater in a sting organized by an informant, Anna Sage, and FBI agents. The movie they watched that day? *Manhattan Melodrama*, starring Clark Gable. Sage, though she actually wore orange and white that day, later became known as the "lady in red."

Al Capone • 1899-1947

Al Capone
Alcatraz mug shot

Al Capone, the son of Italian immigrants, was at the forefront of organized crime in Chicago between 1925 and 1931. His criminal activities involved bootlegging, gambling, and prostitution rings, alongside murdering rivals to expand his territory. Mob violence escalated in Chicago and culminated in the St. Valentine's Day Massacre, during which rival mob members were slaughtered by machine gun fire. Of all the crimes Capone committed, he was finally convicted of tax evasion. As a result, Capone served seven years in prison This included time at Alcatraz. Capone was America's most infamous mob boss and, due to three facial scars, was also known as "Scarface."

Lindbergh kidnapping • March 1, 1932

Aviator Charles Lindbergh's world was turned upside down when his infant son, Charles Jr., was kidnapped. The kidnapper left a note demanding a large ransom, and the nation listened via radio as the horrifying case unfolded. Despite efforts to ransom the child, he was murdered. Circumstantial evidence indicated that a German immigrant named Bruno Hauptmann was guilty of the crime. He was convicted and executed.

Alcatraz • August 16, 1934-1963

On this day, the infamous federal prison located off the coast of California in San Francisco Bay received its first prisoners. The maximum security penitentiary was also known as "the Rock" and home to the U.S.' most violent felons. Famous prisoners held within its walls included Al Capone, Alvin "Creepy Karpis" Karpis, George "Machine Gun" Kelly, and Robert "Birdman of Alcratraz" Stroud. Its isolated location made it expensive to maintain, and as a result, it was closed.

Alcatraz Federal Prison - NASA Satellite Photo

Senator Huey Long's assassination • September 1935

Huey P. Long, a Louisiana senator sometimes called the "Kingfish," was shot and killed. Simultaneously, his bodyguards killed Carl Weiss, a doctor they believed had shot Long. To this day, the incident is shrouded in mystery. Long, formerly a successful lawyer, had served as the state's governor from 1928 until he was elected its senator in 1932. Long had many enemies but was regarded as someone who could have competed with FDR during the next presidential election.

George "Machine Gun" Kelly • 1897-1954

"Machine Gun" Kelly was born George Kelly Barnes. He became involved in crime and married a woman named Kathryn Thorne in 1927. Kelly would go on to become one of the most famous Prohibition-era gangsters, and his new wife Kathryn fostered his "Machine Gun Kelly" image. He was named the FBI's "Public Enemy Number 1." Kelly was arrested after the kidnapping and ransom of Charles Urschel and spent the duration of his life in prison, including time in Alcatraz.

Robert Stroud • 1890-1963

Known as the "Birdman of Alcatraz," Stroud was a criminal whose life in prison began when he was sentenced to 12 years for murder. Time after time, he proved to be violent and deadly even behind prison walls. The murder of a guard ensured that he would never leave confinement again; after receiving a letter from the criminal's mother pleading for Stroud's life to be saved, President Woodrow Wilson himself altered Stroud's sentence from death by hanging to life in solitary confinement. The Birdman earned his nickname when he picked up ornithology, or the study of birds, and took that study with him when he was moved to Alcatraz. Interestingly enough, he even published a book on the diseases of birds.

Alvin Karpis • 1907-1979

Also known as "Creepy Karpis," this Depression-era gangster was classified by the FBI as America's most wanted. He was the son of Lithuanian immigrants and wanted for burglary, bank heists, auto thefts, kidnapping, and murder. FBI Director J. Edgar Hoover himself was at the raid in New Orleans, Louisiana, where Karpis, the last major gangster of his era, was captured in 1936.

HOLLYWOOD'S "GOLDEN AGE"

The "Golden Age" of Hollywood

The **"talkie"** era began at the end of the 1920s, when technological advances permitted for a shift from these silent productions to films with soundtracks. The first feature-length talkie film with dialogue was ***The Jazz Singer*** (1927). A new era in film was begun, and the rise of talkie films signaled a fall in popularity of silent films and vaudeville shows. Celebrities of this era were glamorous, and everyone hit Hollywood, a neighborhood in Los Angeles, California, searching for a big break in show business. Metro-Goldwyn-Mayer (MGM) was the leading film studio.

Snow White and the Seven Dwarfs
December 21, 1937

This was Walt Disney's first full-length feature film and also the first animated in English and technicolor. The story of Snow White was adapted from a Brothers Grimm fairy tale and was immensely successful.

Wizard of Oz poster - MGM

Wizard of Oz • August 1939

Based on stories written by **L. Frank Baum**, this film is about a girl who is whisked to a magical land by a tornado and the series of adventures she endures in order to return home. The film's lead character, Dorothy Gale, was played by Judy Garland. Though it is a popular classic film, it was originally a box office failure. It was one of the first films produced in color and is now a perennial classic.

Judy Garland • 1922-1969

Garland was a singer and actress characterized as talented but troubled. She is best known for her roles in *The Wizard of Oz*, for which she won an Academy Award, and *Meet Me in Saint Louis* (1944).

Gone with the Wind • December 15, 1939

This film was a romantic Civil War saga starring Vivien Leigh as Scarlett O'Hara and Clark Gable as Rhett Butler. The film was based on a Pulitzer Prize-winning novel written by **Margaret Mitchell**. It was one of the earliest color films and remains one of the most popular films of all time.

Clark Gable & Jean Harlow - MGM

Clark Gable • 1901-1960

Clark Gable, also known as the "King of Hollywood," starred in many Hollywood films alongside big names in the industry like Jean Harlow, Greta Garbo, and Norma Shearer. His most famous role was that of Rhett Butler in *Gone with the Wind*. He was known for playing very masculine characters. While one of the most popular Hollywood actors of the era, he was turned down by Hollywood studios early in his acting career because they believed his ears were too large for him to play a starring role.

Bette Davis • 1908-1989

After several Broadway acts and losing a film contract with Universal, Davis was picked up by Warner Brothers. She came to be known as the "First Lady of the American Screen" and was infamous for her volatile personality. Joan Crawford was one of her chief rivals.

Shirley Temple • 1928-2014

This Californian became one of the era's most famous child stars, known for her dimpled smile and blonde curls. She starred in musicals and was a Hollywood box-office sensation, known for hits like "On the Good Ship Lollipop" and movies like *Bright Eyes* (1934) and *Curly Top* (1935). Her popularity waned in the 1940s.

Gary Cooper • 1901-1961

Cooper's family owned a large ranch in Montana, giving him an opportunity to learn horsemanship. He was an aspiring cartoonist and moved to Los Angeles, California, in 1924 during an era when the American public was fascinated by Hollywood western films. Due to his background with horses, he was hired on as an extra and soon graduated to stuntman, cowboy, and then leading roles. His first lead role was in *The Virginian* (1929). Cooper was a substantial influence on many future western actors.

Fred Astaire • 1899-1987

Astaire was an elegant dancer, schooled in the art of dance from childhood, and danced his way to performances not only on stage but in American motion pictures. His best-known roles were in 1930s comedies aside Hollywood starlet Ginger Rogers, with whom he had a great chemistry. Many of Astaire and Roger's dances in these films were tap and ballroom routines.

Gene Autry • 1907-1998

After laboring on railroads and a stint as a telegrapher, this Texan became a best-selling country singer and one of Hollywood's most famous singing cowboys. In Western films, he typically played the heroic character in a white hat riding his horse, Champion. During the course of his music career, he wrote more than 200 songs. He was also a successful entrepreneur and owned several broadcast stations and a baseball team — the Anaheim Angels. Autry was awarded five stars on the Walk of Fame in Hollywood.

ARCHITECTURE

Hoover Dam • 1930-1935

Originally called Boulder Dam, this structure not only stemmed the flow of the Colorado River but diverted water to the Southwest. As a result, it allowed for the development of cities like Los Angeles, Las Vegas, and Phoenix and, to this day, generates electricity for millions of people. The diversion also created Lake Mead and caused the Colorado River to no longer reach the Gulf of California. This structure was completed in 1935 and is the nation's tallest concrete arch dam.

Empire State Building • 1930-1931

Recall the iconic scene in *King Kong* (1933) where the enormous ape climbs a skyscraper with a damsel in distress in tow? The Empire State Building was the setting of this scene and countless other cinematic moments. Located in Midtown Manhattan in New York City, it was designed in the distinctive Art Deco style. Without the additional height of its antennae, it stands 1,250 feet tall; this temporarily captured it the title of "world's tallest building." Miraculously, the enormous structure was built in less than a year. The Empire State Building was dedicated by President Herbert Hoover in 1931.

Golden Gate Bridge • 1933-1937

Construction on this San Francisco suspension bridge, an Art Deco design by Joseph Strauss which crosses the mouth of San Francisco Bay, began in 1933 and was completed in 1937. Though it was an expensive project, it was marketed as an opportunity to create jobs during the Great Depression. At the time of its completion, it was the longest bridge on the planet. This massive and treacherous undertaking replaced the ferry service between San Francisco, California, and Marin County near Sausalito, California.

Frank Lloyd Wright • 1867-1959

Wright was one of America's most influential and innovative modern architects and an interior designer, author, and educator, as well. His building philosophy was centered around the concept of **organic architecture**, or the idea that architecture "should be suited to its environment and be a product of its place, purpose, and time." He designed a bold style which was influenced by the flat landscapes of the Midwest that came to be known as "**Prairie style**" and was influential in U.S. residential design during the 1900s. Homes built in this fashion were constructed from mass-produced materials by mass-produced equipment and were characterized by plain walls and spacious living rooms. Some of Wright's crowning architectural achievements included the **Guggenheim Museum** in New York and **Fallingwater** in Pennsylvania.

Fallingwater residence by Frank Lloyd Wright

LITERATURE

William Faulkner • 1897-1962

Faulkner was a Southerner from Mississippi. In 1918, he enlisted in the British Royal Air Force, but the armistice arrived before he saw combat in WWI. He wrote short stories and novels, his first successful book being set in Mississippi and titled *The Sound and the Fury* (1929). His next success, which was also set in his home state, was *As I Lay Dying* (1930). Faulkner's works were often technically innovative and psychologically powerful. He won the Nobel Prize for Literature in 1949.

Zora Neale Hurston • c. 1891-1960

Hurston was in New York City at the time of the Harlem Renaissance and joined the movement. In 1928, she graduated with a degree in anthropology from Barnard College. She was Barnard College's first African-American graduate and became the first African-American scholar to conduct research on folklore to the depth and extent that she explored. Her writing was characterized by the use of dialects and folk speech and depicted the experience and culture of African Americans living in the rural South. One of her most influential works was *Their Eyes Were Watching God* (1937).

The Yearling • 1938

This Pulitzer Prize-winning novel was written by Marjorie Kinnan Rawlings. It is about a boy and a fawn, or young deer, that he adopts. The story takes place in the forests of Central Florida.

Migrant Mother by Dorothea Lange
Library of Congress

Dorothea Lange • 1895-1965

Lange is best known for her photography and depiction of the plight of people escaping the Dust Bowl and the dire poverty in which they lived. Many of these portraits, which had been published in papers and magazines, are in a book titled *An American Exodus* (1939). Her ability to capture "feeling" in a picture has made her one of the most respected pioneers of documentary photography in the field. Her most well-known photograph, *Migrant Mother* (1936), is on display in the Library of Congress.

Robert L. Ripley • 1890-1949

Ripley was many things, including a cartoonist, explorer, radio personality, movie star, and author. He traveled the globe to find unusual, exotic artifacts and stories. These stories were fodder for a very popular cartoon feature Ripley wrote called "Believe it or Not!" that eventually ran in newspapers across the U.S. In 1933, he opened the first of his carnival-like exhibits, or Odditoriums, at Chicago's World's Fair to showcase his finds. His first books were published in 1929 and 1931 and, due to their success, he began a series

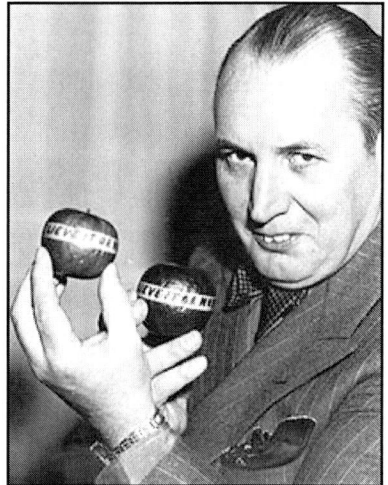

Robert Ripley

of radio broadcasts that would run from 1930 to 1944. He began hosting his own television show in 1949. Ripley died that year but left a very successful company and legacy behind. He popularized the phrase "Believe it or not!" and was known as the "Modern Marco Polo."

Superman • 1938

The first comic featuring Superman was released on this date. The main character was created by two second-generation European Jewish immigrants, Joe Shuster and Jerry Siegel. **DC Comics** purchased the rights to the superhero and began to publish his story; the rest is history. Some argue that the release of Superman initiated the golden age of comics, during which Americans looked to superheroes.

Pearl S. Buck • 1892-1973

Buck's mother and father were Southern Presbyterian missionaries, and she was raised in China. Though she attended college in the U.S., Buck returned to China. Her novels often depict Asian culture and the confrontation between the cultures of the East and West. *The Good Earth* (1931) was her second novel and the first in a trilogy about the Wang family. The novel won a Pulitzer Prize. In 1938, she was awarded the Nobel Prize for Literature. She later established an adoption agency for Asian-American children and took an interest in the welfare of children with special needs.

John Steinbeck • 1902-1968

Steinbeck was an American author. His best-known novels and novellas include *The Grapes of Wrath* (1939), *Of Mice and Men* (1937), and *East of Eden* (1952). *The Grapes of Wrath*, arguably his most famous work, was set during the Great Depression and Dust Bowl. It exposed the conditions endured by migrant farmworkers during this era. He won a Pulitzer Prize for this work, and it was later adapted into a film. Steinbeck was bestowed a Nobel Prize for Literature in 1962. Many of the works he wrote during this era, which primarily explored working-class themes and the natural world, have been cited as his legacy.

SPORTS

Jesse Owens, 1936 - Acme News Photos

Berlin Olympics • 1936

Berlin, Germany, was the host of the 11th Summer Olympics. At this time, the Nazi regime dominated Germany, and other nations considered boycotting the Olympics. The boycott did not happen, and Germany tried to keep its militarism and racism under wraps for the duration of the competition in order to promote a strong, peaceful, and tolerant image. However, Germany prohibited all of its Jewish athletes from competing, save a fencer named Helene Meyer. During these Olympic games, Adolf Hitler promoted Aryans as the ideal athletes. **Jesse Owens**, an African-American track star, proved Hitler wrong by taking home not one but four gold medals. Germany, however, took home the most medals.

Joe Louis • 1914-1981

Louis, whose parents were Alabama sharecroppers, reigned as the world boxing heavyweight champion for 12 years (1937-1949). Perhaps his most famous matches were those fought against German boxer Max Schmeling, as they occurred in the years leading up to World War II and were viewed by some as German Nazism versus American democracy. As a result, Louis' knockout of Schmeling propelled him the status of an American hero. His celebrity status made him a popular icon for African Americans.

Baseball Hall of Fame • 1939

The first baseball "Hall of Fame" class, which included Babe Ruth and others, was inducted in 1939, in honor of baseball's centennial celebration.
The Baseball Hall of Fame was constructed in Cooperstown, New York. Cooperstown was the place where Abner Doubleday, a man who was formerly believed to have invented the American pastime, was reputed to have developed the idea.

SIGNIFICANT NAMES & EVENTS

Discovery of Pluto • February 18, 1930

Percival Lowell believed that the orbits of Uranus and Neptune indicated the existence of another planet. On this day, what was believed to be the ninth planet in our solar system was discovered by a scientist named Clyde Tombaugh at Lowell Observatory in Arizona. While Pluto has since been declared a dwarf planet, it is named for a Greek god, in this case the god of the underworld, like the planets of our solar system. Walt Disney added a character named Pluto to his animated cast of animated characters.

U.S. flag (48 stars), 1931

"The Star-Spangled Banner" March 3, 1931

This song's lyrics were penned by Francis Scott Key. Key was an amateur poet and was inspired to write these verses after watching the American flag fly over Fort McHenry following its bombardment by the British during the War of 1812. In 1931, this song became the nation's national anthem with President Hoover and Congress' approval.

Earhart's solo transatlantic flight • 1932

In May 1932, Amelia Earhart became the first aviatrix — female aviator — to complete a solo transatlantic flight. She continued to fly and set records. The publicity she generated was not only a victory for the advancement of women in American society but also encouraged interest in the development of commercial flights. Earhart attempted to fly across the globe in 1937. Both she and her navigator, Fred Noonan, mysteriously vanished over the Central Pacific during this journey.

Chicago World's Fair
1933-1934

This fair was held in celebration of a "Century of Progress." The city of Chicago's centennial anniversary and new technological and scientific discoveries were celebrated through a series of exhibitions.

Madison Square Garden Riot • February 16, 1934

In New York City, New York, during a rally protesting the massacre of 1,000 socialists in Austria by its fascist leader, Engelbert Dollfuss, a riot between communists and socialists ensued.

Founding of Alcoholics Anonymous • 1935

The roots of Alcoholics Anonymous, or AA, can be found in a recovery meeting that took place in Akron, Ohio. The group developed a book and 12-step program to help alcoholics and other addicts through recovery and has grown to become a global organization, operating on the belief that alcoholism is a disease.

New London School, TX explosion • March 18, 1937

New London, a wealthy oilfield town in East Texas, was rocked by an unprecedented disaster in March 1937. Unaware that there was a natural gas leak, a New London schoolteacher turned on some sanding equipment. This ignited a fire and explosion, ultimately decimating the school. About two hundred and ninety-eight students and teachers were killed, and many more suffered serious injuries. Within weeks of the explosion, the Texas Legislature mandated that thiols, a chemical compound that smells like rotten eggs, be added to natural gas to give it a detectable odor.

Hindenburg disaster • May 6, 1937

Zeppelins, named after their inventor Count Ferdinand von Zeppelin, were created by the Germans and first successfully flown in 1900. In 1937, a German rigid airship, or dirigible, filled with hydrogen burst into flames above Lakehurst, New Jersey. The explosion of this commercial airship, which traveled between Nazi Germany and the United States, resulted in the deaths of 36 people. It was the largest dirigible ever built.

Hindenburg explosion - U.S. Navy

War of the Worlds • October 30, 1938

On this day, **Orson Welles** gave his debut radio broadcast, an adaptation of H.G. Wells' book, *War of the Worlds* (1898). The novel's topic was a Martian invasion of Earth. The broadcast was given a prime time radio slot — Sunday evening — and millions of Americans tuned in. Some thought the dramatized performance was true and panicked, not realizing it was a fictional work. The news media ran with the story to create an image of mass panic that exaggerated the reality. The publicity stunt is notable for sparking Welles' career in Hollywood.

New York City's World's Fair • April 30, 1939-1940

Held in Queens, the theme of this World's Fair was "The World of Tomorrow." Though previous World's Fairs held in major cities across the world had served as a celebration of technological, scientific, and medical progress, this exposition thematically focused on the future. It occurred during the Great Depression but was the second-largest World's Fair in American history.

Norman Rockwell • 1894-1978

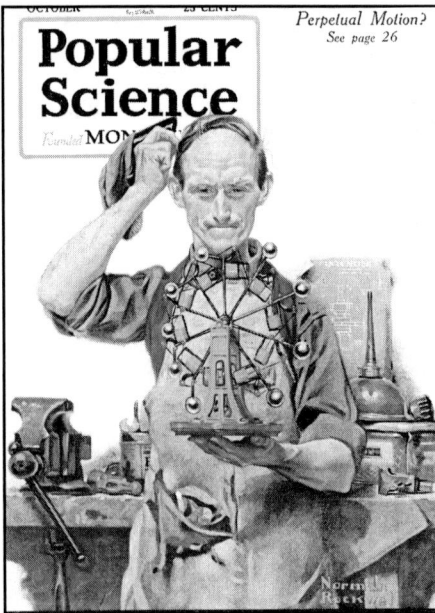

Popular Science cover by Norman Rockwell

Rockwell began to work as a freelance artist for magazines at a very young age and established a long artistic career. He is best remembered for humorous illustrations of family and small-town living. He received the Presidential Medal of Freedom from Gerald R. Ford in 1977. His pieces are still used in art and advertisement today. The term "Rockwellian" has come to denote quaint and old-fashioned sentiments and idealized views of daily life.

TRIVIA

NOTABLE NAMES OF THE 1930s

"Baby Face" Nelson, Charles "Pretty Boy" Floyd, Norma Shearer, Jean Harlow, Marcel Breuer, Benny Goodman, Bing Crosby, Fletcher Henderson, Henry Fonda, Marx brothers, Cary Grant, Vivien Leigh, Errol Flynn, Irene Dunne, Ginger Rogers, Billie Holiday, Count Basie, Glenn Miller

Innovations of the Period:
Monopoly

"I have traveled 201 countries and the strangest thing I saw was man."
– **Robert L. Ripley**

What is polio?

Marx Brothers

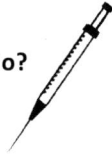

STICKY SITUATIONS

Scotch Tape was invented in 1930 by an engineer named Richard Drew. It was created during the Great Depression, and thus, it became a way for people to make simple and cheap repairs. Scotch still exists today and has created over 400 kinds of adhesive tape.

1930-1939

Dust Bowl Days

The Dust Bowl severely harmed the ecosystems in Plains states and resulted in hordes of jackrabbits and grasshoppers. This grasshopper infestation was so destructive that the National Guard burned fields and squashed the insects with tractors.

FLASH GORDON

In April 1935, the radio saga that captivated Americans made its debut.

Alex Raymond created the science fiction comic strip Flash Gordon in 1934. Universal also adapted this into serial films starring Buster Crabbe. This story is cited as George Lucas' inspiration for *Star Wars*. Other popular serials filmed in the latter half of the 1930s included *Dick Tracy* and *Buck Rogers*.

During Prohibition, Americans found many creative ways to skirt alcohol legislation. Some dive bars did so by charging an entry fee to view a show or animal on display...and providing customers with a complimentary drink. These bars were called "blind pigs."

Though his criminal counterparts called him "Big Fellow" and his friends called him "Snorky," the press called Chicago gangster Al Capone "Scarface." He reportedly despised the moniker.

Batman • March 30, 1939

The company that created Superman, National Comics (now known as DC Comics), introduced a new superhero. Its main character was Bruce Wayne, a vigilante crime-fighter who becomes Batman when he dons his signature costume. This first appearance, Detective Comics # 27, was illustrated by Bob Kane and written by Bill Finger.

1966 Batmobile
Photo - Jennifer Graylock (fordfe.com)

Though the 18th Amendment was repealed by the 21st Amendment, "dry" counties where liquor cannot be sold still exist today. How? Though this amendment ended the federal ban, it did not give the people the constitutional right to transport, sell, or manufacture liquor. Therefore, this can still be limited at the state, county, or city level.

Disney created **Donald Duck** in 1934. The tempermental character made his debut in a short, animated film titled *The Wise Little Hen*. Voice actor Clarence "Ducky" Nash gave life to the animated character from 1934 to 1983. Interestingly enough, Donald has a star on Hollywood's Walk of Fame in Los Angeles, California.

CHAPTER 5

World War II

1940-1949

CONTEXT

As this decade opened, the war overseas was raging.

Measures installed to prevent another global war had proven to be a failure. The humiliating War Guilt Clause and harsh terms of the Treaty of Versailles (1918) humiliated and infuriated the German people. Under these conditions, Adolf Hitler, a painter who served in the German army during WWI, rose to lead the National Socialist German Workers' Party (Nazi Party) and was appointed chancellor of Germany.

World War II (WWII) started as two separate wars, one in Asia and the other in Europe. WWII in Asia officially began when Japan invaded China on July 7, 1937. After the Japanese captured much of Northeastern China, the conflict bogged into a stalemate with neither side making decisive gains.

In Europe, the war began in 1939, when Germany invaded Poland and pulled England and France into the fray. Hitler launched a *blitzkrieg*, or *lightning war*, and occupied much of Europe between 1939 and 1941. Stymied in his efforts to conquer Britain, Hitler invaded the Soviet Union (USSR) on June 22, 1941. U.S. sympathies lay with France and Great Britain, though the American people did not want to join the war efforts. The U.S. maintained its neutral stance, and the war overseas continued to escalate. This neutrality began to waver.

The Germans advanced across Europe, attacking and conquering Denmark, Norway, Belgium, the Netherlands, and France. The U.S. provided aid and supplies to Britain and members of the Allies. Japan proved to be the deciding factor, bombing Pearl Harbor and "waking the sleeping giant" after it perceived the U.S. as the only major remaining threat to its goals to build an Asian empire.

The U.S. joined the Allies as Britain and the USSR were staving off the German advance, bolstering their war efforts. They also engaged the Japanese, taking the lead in operations in the Pacific. Americans began rationing supplies and stepped up production, shifting to a wartime economy. The Allies were victorious.

After the war, occupation planted the seeds of the Cold War between the USSR and the United States.

PRESIDENTS & ELECTIONS

Election of 1940 • November 5, 1940

Franklin D. Roosevelt ran for reelection, seeking his third term in office. He won the popular vote by almost five million votes and dominated the electoral vote, soundly beating his opponent, Republican candidate Wendell L. Willkie. Roosevelt was the first U.S. president elected to a third term in office, breaking the tradition set by George Washington for presidents to voluntarily step down after two terms. Henry A. Wallace would serve as his new vice president, replacing John Nance Garner.

Election of 1944 • November 7, 1944

Franklin D. Roosevelt did not stop at his third term; he went on to run for a fourth in this election. As was the case in the Election of 1940, the primary concern was each candidate's disposition and ability to handle the war overseas. Republican Thomas E. Dewey, governor of New York, fell to FDR by a landslide, and Roosevelt took to office for the fourth and final time. Harry S. Truman replaced Henry A. Wallace as vice president.

Roosevelt dies • April 12, 1945

FDR suffered a severe cerebral hemorrhage while posing for a portrait painter and passed away before completing his fourth term in office. He had served as head of the nation through not only the Great Depression but also WWII, two of the nation's most alarming crises. Harry S. Truman, who had served as FDR's vice president, ascended to the presidency and became the commander in chief during WWII.

Harry S. Truman
1884-1972

Truman was born in Lamar, Missouri, and grew up on the family farm in Independence. He never completed college and worked an assortment of jobs. Truman was also a member of the National Guard and volunteered to serve in the American Expeditionary Force overseas during WWI, leading his regiment during the Meuse-Argonne campaign in France.

After WWI, he married Elizabeth "Bess" Wallace. His career in politics was kick-started by the support

Harry S. Truman

of Democratic boss Thomas J. Pendergast. He served as an overseer of highways and then as a judge, earning a reputation for being a capable and honest man of integrity. Pendergast helped him win election to the U.S. Senate in 1934. During WWII, he served as chair of the "Truman Committee," a congressional committee that provided oversight to war production.

He became FDR's running mate in the presidential Election of 1944. Truman abruptly ascended to the presidency at FDR's death, becoming the 33rd president and inheriting the helm of WWII leadership at the end of the conflict. He decided to drop the atomic bombs of Hiroshima and Nagasaki, Japan, effectively wreaking mass destruction on and causing Japan to drop out of the war and ending WWII. His administration dealt with the threat of Soviet expansionism and, in time, the Cold War. His response to this expansionism was the **Truman Doctrine**, which stated that the U.S. would actively oppose communist aggression globally. While in office, he preserved the New Deal, and his domestic reform program was called the **Fair Deal**.

Presidential Succession Act • July 18, 1947

This act was signed by President Truman and made the Speaker of the House next in line (after the vice president) in the event of the president's death or incapacity to serve. It was passed as a result of the succession question raised by FDR's abrupt death.

Election of 1948 • November 2, 1948

Incumbent Democratic president Harry S. Truman ran against Republican candidate Thomas E. Dewey, and Dixiecrat Strom Thurmond. Many did not think Truman had a shot at victory, but he proved them wrong, winning both the popular and electoral votes. Ironically enough, the *Chicago Tribune*, printed a front-page headline reading "DEWEY DEFEATS TRUMAN."

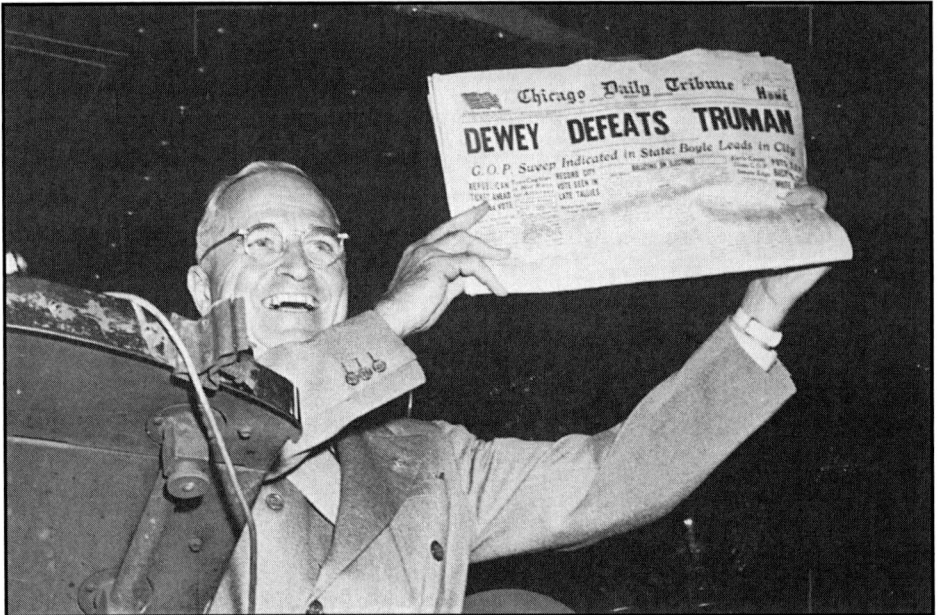

Harry S. Truman holding the *Chicago Tribune* - U.S. Information Agency

WORLD WAR II

This section, like that on WWI, will discuss the war from the American perspective and address several key battles, but by no means all.

U.S. neutrality

While the war raged, the U.S. maintained the neutral stance they had declared through the 1935, 1937, and 1939 Neutrality Acts. The American people sought isolationism and distance from the conflict, which prevented trade and loans to any warring countries. They continued to watch the events unfold overseas.

Naval Expansion Act • June 14, 1940

The German advance across Europe continued, and the president, FDR, signed this act as Paris, France, fell. It enlarged the Navy's capacity by 11 percent, increasing the amount of U.S. naval warships by building vessels like aircraft carriers, submarines, and cruisers. More naval acts would follow, allowing the U.S. to base fleets in two oceans — the Pacific and the Atlantic.

Selective Training and Service Act September 16, 1940

This Congressional legislation was signed by FDR and enacted the nation's first peacetime draft. The decision to begin beefing up the U.S. military was made in the wake of WWII, which was raging overseas, and Japan showing aggression in the Pacific Ocean.

Neutrality Acts & Lend-Lease Act

Isolationist sentiment prompted the passage of the first Neutrality Act in 1935. This legislation, which stated that the U.S. could not export "arms, ammunition, and implements of war" to warring countries, was intended to keep the U.S. from being pulled into wars overseas. The threat of fascism abroad grew, however, and public opinion began to shift. The Neutrality Act of 1937 added "**cash-and-carry**," which permitted the sale of nonmilitary goods to countries at war with the stipulation that the customer paid in cash and the items were not transported by ships registered in the U.S. The Neutrality Act of 1939 kept the cash-and-carry provision, but allowed the U.S. to sell military goods to warring countries. Direct monetary loans to such countries remained prohibited. The **Destroyers for Bases Agreement** between Britain and Roosevelt's administration took advantage of a loophole in this by making a straight trade with Britain. The U.S. sent Britain 30 destroyers, or large naval ships for battle, in return for the right to use some British air and naval bases. When England began to run low on the cash necessary to purchase these items during WWII, the Lend-Lease Act was passed in March 1941. This ended cash-and-carry and allowed the U.S. to send military aid overseas without requiring payment. The Neutrality Act of 1941 specified that U.S. ships could now carry items to warring nations.

U.S. occupation of Iceland • July 7, 1941

In April 1940, Germany invaded Denmark, and Iceland, one of Denmark's states, was left temporarily independent. Britain extended an offer to defend Iceland, which did not have a military force to defend itself. Iceland refused, citing its wish to remain neutral. Britain ignored Iceland's wishes and occupied the country, not only to keep the area from German occupation but to have a base in the North Atlantic. In 1941, the U.S. took over this responsibility, sending soldiers to occupy Iceland.

Pearl Harbor bombed • December 7, 1941

On this date, an American naval base on the Hawaiian island of Oahu was attacked by Japanese bombers. At the time, most of the U.S. Pacific

Fleet was at this location. The Japanese hoped to cripple the U.S.' ability to respond to their conquest of Asia and the Pacific. The attack was unexpected, and approximately 2,500 Americans lost their lives. Nineteen ships, eight of which were battleships, were sunk or sustained significant damage, and many aircraft were obliterated or badly damaged. The date of this attack came to be known as the "Day of Infamy" after a speech made by President FDR. The bombing of Pearl Harbor was the catalyst that drew the U.S. into WWII. The U.S. declared war on Japan the following day.

The U.S. joined the **Allied Powers**, which included Great Britain, France, the Soviet Union, Poland, and China, among others. Opposing them were the **Axis Powers**, comprised of Germany, Japan, Italy, and others.

Japan bombs Pearl Harbor, December 7, 1941

U.S. internment camps • 1942-1946

The Pearl Harbor attack and U.S. entry into WWII fostered widespread anti-Japanese sentiment within the United States. As a result of this paranoia, President FDR signed **Executive Order 9066**, which placed those with Japanese ancestry in internment camps. The constitutionality of this act was challenged by *Korematsu v. United States* (1944), during which the Supreme

Court ruled that the order was constitutional and a wartime necessity. It was not until the late 1980s that Congress took an apologetic stance and awarded those who survived $20,000 each.

Island hopping

Island hopping was a military strategy by which the U.S. hoped to win the war in the Pacific Theatre. B-29 bombers attempted to take back islands from Japanese forces in the region and defeat well-defended islands in the region by isolating them from the rest.

Battle of Midway • June 1942

This battle, which was primarily fought with aircraft via aircraft carriers, occurred in the Pacific Theatre at Midway Atoll after Pearl Harbor. The Japanese fleet, led by Admiral **Yamamoto Isoroku**, planned to sink American destroyers that had not been disabled during the Pearl Harbor attack. This plan was foiled when Americans cracked the Japanese code and interpreted their plans. The commander of the U.S. Pacific Fleet, Admiral **Chester N. Nimitz**, was prepared, and U.S. forces won the battle. This decisive win, combined with the Battle of Guadalcanal, was called a turning point in the Pacific Theatre and allowed the Allies to go on the offensive in this region.

Battle of Guadalcanal • August 1942-February 1943

The Japanese occupied a southern Solomon Island, Guadalcanal, in July and built an airfield. This battle, fought both on land and sea, began when U.S. Marines launched a surprise attack and took the Japanese airfield. The battle was fought in the jungles, but the Japanese were unable to retake the airfield. Naval battles also occurred as both the Allies and Japan tried to ship in reinforcements. In the end, Japan was outnumbered and evacuated its troops.

Second Front Controversy

Joseph Stalin wanted the Allies to open a second front in Western Europe to divert German forces and relieve some of the pressure on the USSR. The British and other Allied leaders were hesitant to do so, suspicious of Stalin and focused on efforts elsewhere, and continually postponed it. When the Soviets began making progress on the Eastern Front in 1943 and it became clear that Germany would be defeated, the Allies agreed to open the second front. It was launched by the invasion of Normandy in 1944.

Invasion of Normandy • June 6, 1944

Dwight D. Eisenhower was named the Supreme Allied Commander. Allied troops invaded the beaches of Normandy in France, pushing to liberate Paris and the rest of western Europe. This invasion, one of the biggest amphibious military operations to date, was also called **Operation Overlord**, and its launch date is also known as **D-Day**. By the end of August, northern France was free of Germany.

G.I. Bill of Rights • June 22, 1944

FDR signed the G.I. Bill of Rights, also known as the Servicemen's Readjustment Act of 1944. This legislation was enacted to offer benefits for WWII veterans through the Veteran's Administration (VA). Some of these benefits included school and college tuition grants, low-interest small-business loans, and low-interest mortgages. It was later amended and extended to all veterans.

Audie Murphy • 1925-1971

Texan Audie Murphy enlisted in the army to serve during WWII. He fought in eight campaigns in Sicily, Italy, France, and Germany and was awarded more medals than any other American combat soldier for his WWII service. Most famously, Murphy was credited with killing about 50 Germans and stopping an attack by enemy tanks during a single skirmish in 1945 in France. He later became a Hollywood star and even played himself in an autobiographical film based on his own memoir, *To Hell and Back* (1955).

Robert Oppenheimer • 1904-1967

Oppenheimer, known as the "father of the atomic bomb," was a brilliant theoretical physicist who worked with quantum theory. He headed the laboratory at Los Alamos, New Mexico, that created and tested the atomic bomb. After the first test bomb exploded, Oppenheimer was astounded. He quoted an excerpt from the Bhagavad Gita which came to mind at the sight of the **Trinity test**: "I am become death: the destroyer of worlds." He later opposed development of the hydrogen bomb.

Manhattan Project 1942-1945

Many believed the Germans were developing an atomic bomb. American scientists, a large number of whom had escaped fascist European states, convinced **Albert Einstein** to contact President FDR and express the military significance of researching

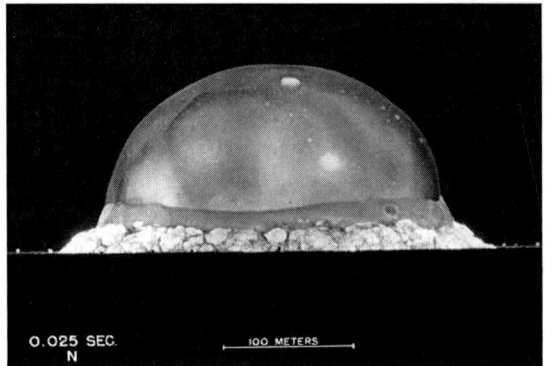

"Trinity Test" at Alamogordo Test Range - U.S. Government

uncontrolled fission chain reactions in 1939. The government research project was undertaken by military director General Leslie Groves and scientific director of the **Los Alamos Laboratory**, or **Project Y**, the New Mexico lab where this research was undertaken, Robert Oppenheimer. The first plutonium bomb was successfully tested on July 16, 1945 at a test site on the Alamogordo air base in New Mexico. This test is known as the **Trinity Test**. In order to end the war with Japan, President Truman opted to drop atomic bombs called "Little Boy" and "Fat Man" on the Japanese cities of Hiroshima and Nagasaki the following month.

146

Battle of the Bulge • December 1944-January 1945

The Germans launched a desperate surprise counterattack in northwest Europe. Their objective was to make a blitzkrieg-style advance through the Ardennes, a rugged and heavily forested region, to Antwerp and split the Allied forces. American units were surprised and fought to hold the line. It took on a bulge-like form, thus the battle's name. Lieutenant George S. Patton's repositioning of the Third Army to counterattack, the Americans' valiant fight, and a shortage of fuel in the German lines led to an Allied victory. The Battle of the Bulge, or the Battle of Ardennes, was the final large German offensive mounted during WWII.

Yalta Conference • February 4-11, 1945

This conference was held in Yalta, Crimea, and included the primary members of the Allied leadership — FDR, British Prime Minister Winston Churchill, and Soviet Premier Joseph Stalin. Allied leadership was sure of victory in Europe but sought Soviet assistance in the Pacific and Soviet enrollment in the new United Nations (UN). The primary objective of the Yalta Conference was to plan Germany's defeat and occupation, alongside a course of action to deal with defeated or liberated Eastern European countries after the war. The West's decision to accept Stalin's promise that he would allow democratic regimes in Eastern Europe became a controversy and set the stage for the impending Cold War.

Battle of Iwo Jima • February 19-March 26, 1945

Iwo Jima is a volcanic island located in the Bonin chain that is about 750 miles away from the Japanese city of Tokyo. U.S. forces needed a base close to Japan. They bombed this area by sea and air, then launched an amphibious invasion. Rather than defending the coastline, the Japanese concentrated their troops inland and fought from a series of caves, dugouts, and tunnels. A month-long battle ensued, and the U.S. was victorious. Of the approximately 21,000 Japanese troops at this location, roughly 1,000 survived.

Photograph of flag raising on Iwo Jima
Photo by Joe Rosenthal - U.S. Archives

Nazi surrender • May 7, 1945

In March 1945, the Allies invaded Germany proper and conquered it a few months after Hitler committed suicide in Berlin. German leaders agreed to 'unconditional surrender,' accepting complete Allied occupation. Germany surrendered in May 1945.

Potsdam Conference • July 17-August 2, 1945

Allied leadership met outside of Berlin — Potsdam, Germany. Harry S. Truman, Joseph Stalin, Winston Churchill, and new British Prime Minister Clement Atlee convened to determine how to navigate the peace settlements in Europe. Some of their concerns included how to administrate Germany, Polish boundaries, Austrian occupation, the Soviet relationship with Eastern Europe, and winning the war against Japan. This included a decision to divide Germany into four administrative parts, managed by the U.S., Soviet Union, Britain, and France respectively.

Japanese surrender • September 2, 1945

To save American lives, President Truman sought a way to quickly and decisively end the war without invading Japan. In the summer of 1945, he made the decision to drop atomic bombs on Japan. In August, the bombs were dropped on the cities of Hiroshima and Nagasaki and killed around 140,000 Japanese citizens almost instantly. Japan surrendered informally August 1945, just weeks after the bombings, and delivered an official surrender in September.

THE COLD WAR

Cold War

Though the U.S. and the Soviet Union (USSR) both fought as members of the Allied Powers during WWII, relations between the two countries began to deteriorate during the Potsdam Conference and joint occupation of Germany. The Soviets expanded their influence in Eastern Europe, creating communist governments in Poland, Hungary, Bulgaria, Czechoslovakia, Romania, Albania, and East Germany. Meanwhile, the U.S. departed from its policy of nonintervention in European affairs and sought to prevent the spread of communism and contain it. The Cold War dragged on for 45 years, ending around 1991.

Truman Doctrine • March 12, 1947

On this date, President Harry S. Truman gave a speech to Congress stating that the U.S. must aid democracies threatened by communist domination and asked Congress to aid Greece and Turkey (Great Britain had recently announced that they would no longer be doing so). After the Soviet Union enforced communist dictatorships over its occupied countries in Eastern Europe, the Truman administration perceived the spread of communism as a matter of national security and decided to "take a stand" against the Soviet Union. Truman asked for $400 million in aid to Turkey and Greece. In essence, the Truman Doctrine defined American foreign policy during the Cold War and was a departure from its former tendency of nonintervention in conflicts that did not directly involve the U.S.

Containment

George Kennan, a Foreign Service officer, was stationed in the USSR. In 1946, he transmitted a lengthy message called the "Long Telegram" which described Joseph Stalin's regime's foreign policy, and in 1947, he also published an anonymous piece in *Foreign Affairs*. Kennan believed the best way to handle the aggressive Soviet policy was to "contain" its expansion over time. Containment was adopted as a U.S. foreign policy for the end of the forties and early fifties.

Central Intelligence Agency (CIA) established 1947

Established by the provisions of the National Security Act of 1947, this organization was created to collect, correlate, evaluate, and disseminate intelligence for national security purposes. Truman deemed its conception a necessity due to national security concerns relating to the USSR and Cold War.

Marshall Plan • April 1948-December 1951

George C. Marshall, U.S. secretary of state, issued a call to aid Europe after WWII. The resulting plan passed by Congress helped rebuild Western Europe's economy, but also served to create a venue for American goods, helping the U.S. economy. The plan also intended to create a contrast between the U.S. treatment of Western Europe and Soviet actions in the east. Marshall was later awarded a Nobel Prize for his effort to create peace.

Organization of American States (OAS) April 30, 1948

After WWII, a charter signed by the U.S. and 20 Latin American nations created the OAS. Its goal was to foster improved political relations between these countries. The U.S. had another goal — to prevent the spread of communism into its hemisphere; hence, a phrase condemning communism and totalitarianism was included in the agreement. This charter followed the Rio Act, which established a military alliance between these countries. Overall, the OAS did not meet the expectations of the U.S. or Latin American nations.

Alger Hiss indicted • December 15, 1948

Alger Hiss, 1950
Library of Congress

A communist named Whittaker Chambers accused Hiss, a State Department official, of being a Soviet spy who disclosed top secret reports. This intelligence was called the "Pumpkin Papers," because — you guessed it — Chambers stashed the documents in one of the big, orange gourds. Hiss was not charged with treason, due to the statute of limitations, but with perjury. While the 1949 court case resulted in a hung jury, he was given a guilty sentence in a second trial in 1950 and spent several years in jail. This controversial court case fascinated the nation.

NATO established • April 4, 1949

After WWII, Soviet armies remained in both Central and Eastern Europe. In response to the perceived Soviet threat, the North Atlantic Treaty Organization (NATO) was established. This military alliance included the U.K., Canada, Belgium, France, Luxembourg, Iceland, Denmark, Italy, the Netherlands, Portugal, Norway, and the U.S. and later expanded to include other nations. This agreement is also referred to as the Washington Treaty. It established that every member would support any other member that came under armed assault.

INVENTIONS & INNOVATIONS

Jeep

In the early 1940s, during WWII, the U.S. Army sought a design for a lightweight, all-terrain reconnaissance vehicle. They asked automobile manufacturers to create a prototype meeting these requirements and gave them a 49-day deadline. Bantam Car Company called in Karl Probst, an engineer from Detroit, to help them meet the deadline. Willys and Ford companies created prototypes based off of Bantam's designs, and the Willys Quad won the contract. Ford was brought into the fray when the company granted the U.S. government the authority to allow another company to produce the vehicle to satisfy demand.

ENIAC • February 14, 1946

From 1943 to 1945, programmers worked to design a computer for the war effort. Their design, which was not completed and sent to the Army until after the war was over, was called the Electronic Numerical Integrator and Computer (ENIAC). This revolutionary machine was the first general-purpose electronic computer and could quickly complete difficult and time-consuming calculations. The machine was enormous and weighed over 30 tons — compare that to today's handheld smartphones! The government revealed it to the public in 1946.

Sound barrier broken • October 14, 1947

To break the sound barrier, a pilot must fly faster than the speed of sound itself. And that's exactly what U.S. Air Force Captain Chuck Yeager did in an X-1 plane called the *Glamourous Glennis*.

SPORTS & ATHLETES

Joe DiMaggio • 1914-1999

Marilyn Monroe & Joe DiMaggio, 1954 - *Now* magazine

This baseball star acquired legendary status playing for the New York Yankees for 13 years (1936-1951), the entirety of his Major League career. During that time, the team won nine World Series. DiMaggio was also known as the "Yankee Clipper" and took an almost three-year leave during the height of his baseball career to serve in the Army during WWII. In 1941, DiMaggio had an impressive hitting streak that lasted 56 games. For a short period of time, he was married to legendary actress **Marilyn Monroe**. He became a Baseball Hall of Fame inductee in 1955.

Basketball Association of America founded June 6, 1946

WWII was over, and American leisure activities could resume. Until 1936, professional basketball had a bad reputation and had been unsuccessful, though college basketball fared well and flourished during WWII. The Basketball Association of America was founded in 1946 but merged with the National Basketball League in 1949 to become the **National Basketball Association** (NBA) we know today.

MLB integration • April 15, 1947

Segregation was not officially written into MLB rules, but it was evident on the field. Renowned baseball star and veteran Jackie Robinson became the first African American to play in the Major League when he made his debut with the Brooklyn Dodgers in 1945.

Jackie Robinson - Library of Congress

Yogi Berra • 1925-2015

Lawrence Peter Berra was given his famous moniker, "Yogi," as a teenager. Like DiMaggio, Berra played for the New York Yankees. He spent 18 years with the team (1946-1963) and played in an astonishing 14 World Series, 10 of which the Yankees won. In 1972, he was given a place in the Baseball Hall of Fame. The baseball great is also remembered for his hilarious, and often nonsensical, one-liners. Here are a few favorites attributed to Berra:

- *"It ain't over till it's over."*
- *"Little League baseball is a very good thing because it keeps the parents off the streets."*
- *"The future ain't what it used to be."*

SWING ERA

Swing and big bands • 1935-mid-1940s

This style of music was a derivation of jazz with a rhythmic drive and "call and response" between sections. More members were involved in swing groups (roughly anywhere between 12 to 16 musicians) than in traditional jazz groups. These bands included brass, reeds, and rhythm sections. Fletcher Henderson, an African-American pianist, was one of its pioneering arrangers, and Duke Ellington was one of its most famous. Swing lent respect to jazz and was the first kind of jazz that proved to be a commercial success.

Jitterbug

This form of ballroom dance was in 4/4 time with a syncopated rhythm and popular during the 1930s and 1940s. Though it originated in the U.S., it became a global sensation when American soldiers popularized the style during WWII. Couples typically held either one or both hands and incorporated acrobatic swings and lifts while doing footwork like the lindy hop and the jive.

Nat King Cole

Nat King Cole • 1919-1965

Cole was an African-American musician, jazz pianist, and vocalist known for his soft baritone. He later went on to become the first African American to host a variety television show and also tackled roles on the silver screen. Some of his most memorable songs include "Unforgettable," "Mona Lisa," and "Ramblin' Rose."

Bing Crosby • 1903-1977

Harry Lillis Crosby said he acquired the nickname "Bing" due to his love for a comic strip called "The Bingville Bugle." This singer and songwriter was known for his relaxed demeanor and crooning voice. He was popular on the radio and went on to have a successful movie star career. In 1945, he took home an Academy Award for his role in *Going My Way* (1944). He recorded over 300 hit singles, and his versions of "White Christmas" and "Silent Night" became holiday classics, two of the most popular recordings of the 20th century.

Ella Fitzgerald

Ella Fitzgerald • 1917-1996

Fitzgerald was an African-American vocalist noted for her impressive vocal range and billed as "the First Lady of Song." Her recording of "A-Tisket, A-Tasket" was her first Billboard hit. Fitzgerald tackled bebop, scat, and many other styles. During the course of her career, Yale University awarded her a doctorate of music, and she took home a grand total of 13 Grammy Awards.

FILM & ACTORS

Abbott & Costello

Bud Abbott and Lou Costello teamed up to create this dynamic, rapid-fire, slapstick comedic duo in 1936. The comedies they filmed between 1940 and 1956 preserved American vaudeville and burlesque on film.

Film noir • early 1940s-late 1950s

This style of filmmaking hit Hollywood in the early 1940s. They were often characterized by dark settings, shadows, and strange camera angles, alongside their presentation of plots where right and wrong were not cut-and-dried and their lack of happy endings. The French later came upon these films and coined their name. Translated, "film noir" means "dark film."

Pinocchio • February 23, 1940

This musical was Walt Disney Productions' second animated feature film. It was adapted from a children's book called *The Adventures of Pinocchio* written by C. Collodi, and its main character was a living puppet.

Bugs Bunny debut • July 27, 1940

Warner Brothers released an animated cartoon called *A Wild Hare* by Tex Avery. This cartoon was the first appearance of none other than Bugs Bunny, a rabbit known for outsmarting a hunter named Elmer Fudd and his famous catch phrase, "What's up, Doc?"

Orson Welles in *Citizen Kane*

Citizen Kane • 1941

Orson Welles not only co-wrote, directed, and produced this drama, but also served in a leading role. The film is about a publishing tycoon and was, in essence, an attack on publisher William Randolph Hearst. It is famous for its groundbreaking use of lighting, methods of focusing, and dramatic style of editing. The film took home an Academy Award for best screenplay, was nominated for many more, and is often considered to be one of the best masterpieces of cinema to date.

Casablanca • 1942

This iconic American film was set in Morocco during WWII and loosely based on a play by Murray Burnett and Joan Alison called *Everybody Comes to Rick's*. The romance starred Humphrey Bogart and Ingrid Bergman, was a box-office success, and received three Academy Awards.

Frank Capra • 1897-1991

Capra and his family immigrated from Sicily to Los Angeles in 1903. Though he earned a chemical engineering degree from the California Institute of Technology in 1918, he later delved into filmmaking with no experience and worked his way from the bottom to a director at Columbia Pictures. The Italian American is remembered as the key filmmaker of his decade, and his works were characteristically idealistic, patriotic, and sentimental. Capra was the recipient of three Academy Awards for directing. Some of his most famous films include *Mr. Deeds Goes to Town* (1936) and *You Can't Take It With You* (1938). From 1942 to 1945, he also produced seven award-winning WWII propaganda films called *Why We Fight*.

Humphrey Bogart • 1899-1957

Bogart, born in New York City, got his start on Broadway but moved on to act on film, signing with Fox Film Corporation. By the 1940s and 1950s, he was a wildly popular movie star. He was often cast as the "tough guy," and two of his most famous roles were those he played in *The Maltese Falcon* (1941) and *Casablanca* (1942).

Alfred Hitchcock • 1899-1980

Hitchcock, born in Britain, became one of America's leading motion picture directors. In 1920, he entered the industry as an artist, creating title cards for silent films. He later began to direct, and his films and television shows were characterized by suspense and a morbid sense of humor, alongside personal cameos. One of his most popular films is *Psycho* (1960). He moved from Britain to the U.S. in 1940. Hitchcock was knighted in 1979, the year before he died.

Frank Sinatra • 1915-1998

Frank Sinatra
Library of Congress

Sinatra was born in Hoboken, New Jersey, and, inspired by Bing Crosby, wanted to become a pop singer when he grew up. Sinatra was successful in this endeavor and became the most popular singer of this era, known for his crooning baritone voice and black fedora hat. He starred in films and musicals, including *Anchors Aweigh* (1945), *On the Town* (1949), *From Here to Eternity* (1953), *The Manchurian Candidate* (1962), *Ocean's 11* (1960), and many more. Sinatra even became a successful producer.

John Wayne • 1907-1979

John Wayne publicity photo for *The Comancheros*
20th Century Fox

Born Marion Michael Morrison and nicknamed the "Duke," this actor adopted the stage name John Wayne and was typically cast as a tough cowboy or solider. Wayne worked in over 200 films, mostly westerns, during his career. In 1969, he took home an Oscar for his performance in *True Grit* (1969). He remains an American icon.

Jimmy Stewart • 1908-1997

Stewart was an actor known for his portrayal of idealistic, small-town American characters. He acted in many films, but some of his most famous roles were in Frank Capra-directed films like *You Can't Take it With You* (1938), *Mr. Smith Goes to Washington* (1939) and *It's a Wonderful Life* (1946). Interestingly enough, Stewart knew how to fly a plane and, thus, was drafted into the Army around 1940. He served in WWII and Vietnam. *It's A Wonderful Life*, filmed upon his return from WWII, helped to restart his career and made him a star.

Tennessee Williams • 1911-1983

Williams was a successful and prolific American playwright. His first major success was *The Glass Menagerie* (1944), and his next major work was the Pulitzer Prize-winning *A Streetcar Named Desire* (1947). Williams also won a Pulitzer Prize for *Cat on a Hot Tin Roof* (1955).

Roy Rogers • 1911-1998

Lynne Roberts & Roy Rogers in *Billy the Kid Returns*
Republic Pictures

Rogers was known as the "Singing Cowboy" and, like Autry, got his start singing country-western songs on the radio before graduating to film. His movie and television career was a prolific one, and again like Autry, he played the hero in the white hat. In many of these, Autry rode the same horse, Trigger. His signature theme song, which he had recorded with his wife and co-star Dale Evans, was "Happy Trails." Before launching his career in Los Angeles, Rogers' real name was Leonard Franklin Slye.

SIGNIFICANT NAMES & EVENTS

Wonder Woman • December 1941

The adventures of Wonder Woman, an Amazonian with superpowers, were first published by All-American Comics. This character was a step away from the overt masculinity of the comic book industry to date. The author's identity was withheld and surprised the nation when it was revealed through a series of press releases. The invisible enemy of injustice was the brainchild of Dr. William Moulton Marston, a famous psychologist influenced by the early suffrage movement. Interestingly enough, he was also the inventor of the lie detector. Some call Wonder Woman, a feminist icon, the most famous female comic book superhero.

Captain America • March 1941

This comic series was written and illustrated for Timely Comics, a company now known as **Marvel**, by Joe Simon and Jack Kirby. The main character, Steve Rogers, becomes a super-soldier called Captain America by way of a serum and enlists in the Army.

Bob Hope • 1903-2003

Though born in England, Hope's family relocated to the U.S. when he was four years old. Known for his fast jokes, great delivery, and one-liners, Hope was an entertainer and comic actor. He was successful in all major entertainment media of his time — the stage, movies, radio, and television. Hope is also known for devoting much time to performing for troops stationed abroad.

Fertilizer plant explosion • 1947

Ammonium nitrate, an explosive material used during WWII, was also an ingredient in fertilizer. An explosion was ignited while loading fertilizer onto a freighter called the S.S. *Grandcamp* in Texas City, Texas. The ship, a local chemical storage facility, and 500 homes were obliterated. Around 600 were killed, and thousands suffered injuries.

Pentagon • 1941

Construction on the Pentagon began in September 1941 and was completed in January 1943. It is one of the world's largest office buildings and was created to hold members of the War Department (now called the Department of Defense) during WWII.

Rosie the Riveter • 1942

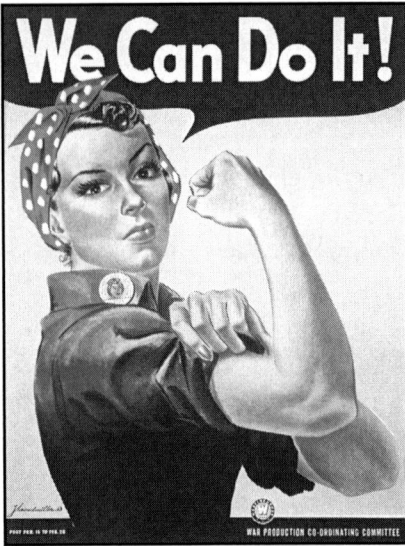

Rosie the Riveter by J. Howard Miller
Virginia Historical Society

As men were drawn overseas to participate in the war efforts, American women stepped into roles that traditionally belonged to men. Most were working-class women, but as time passed, middle-class women were also needed. To encourage this group to join the work force, the U.S. Office of the War churned out propaganda. One such piece of propaganda was Rosie the Riveter, an iconic image of a working woman in a red bandana with her arm flexed and the famous caption "We Can Do It!" The image, created by J. Howard Miller, has since been appropriated for use in many movements. The following year, Redd Evans and John Jacob Loeb released a song titled "Rosie the Riveter," and artist Norman Rockwell created a depiction of her.

Zoot Suit Riots • 1943

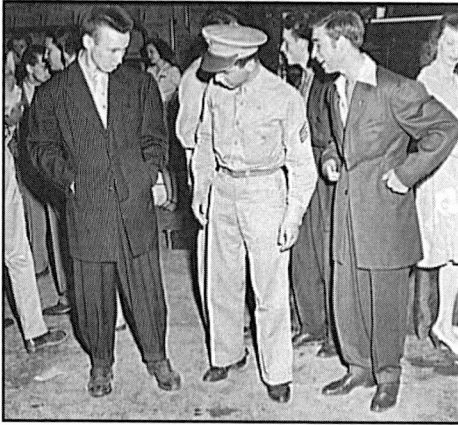

Officer inspecting men in zoot suits, 1942
Library of Congress

Zoot suits were loose suit coats with long tails and high-waisted wool trousers that were popular among Latino youth in Los Angeles. These baggy suits used a lot of material, which was viewed as unpatriotic during the war and an era of rationing, and some servicemen associated the suits with draft dodgers. Racial tension between these Mexican Americans and white sailors and Marines culminated in violent riots where servicemen and civilians attacked not only those wearing the fashion, but also Mexican Americans, Blacks, and Filipinos. The riots took place in June 1943. The city council banned the suits.

All the King's Men • 1946

Robert Penn Warren, a southern poet and novelist, published a political novel called *All the King's Men*. The novel discusses a politician's rise to power in the 1930s, and one of its central themes is human fallibility and political corruption. The central politician discussed in the novel is believed to have been modeled on Senator Huey Long. Interestingly enough, Warren is the only writer to have won Pulitzer Prizes for both his poems and works of fiction.

Black Dahlia • 1947

An aspiring actress named Elizabeth Short was murdered in Los Angeles. Short was called the "Black Dahlia" by friends because of her characteristically dark hair and clothing. Despite the media attention given to the case and numerous bizarre confessions, the crime was never solved. This mystery has been the subject of books, movies, and television specials.

Roswell U.F.O. landing • 1947

A rancher named Mac Brazel outside of Roswell, New Mexico, stumbled on strange, unidentifiable material in his pasture. Brazel contacted the authorities, and soldiers from the Roswell Army Air Force base collected the debris. The event was shrouded in mystery, and some believed that the crashed vehicle was a "flying saucer" and attributed the wreckage to aliens. Though the military maintained that the vehicle was a weather balloon for years, it has declassified materials addressing the event. The documents claim that the debris were from experimental balloons used in the top-secret Project Mogul, an atomic espionage project at Alamogordo Airfield. Regardless, the crash site and nearby town of Roswell attract hundreds of thousands of tourists annually.

Desegregation of the Armed Forces • July 26, 1948

President Harry S. Truman desegregated the U.S. military through **Executive Order 9981** after Southern Senate members prevented the action from being passed by Congress. At this point in time, African Americans made up approximately 10 percent of the American population. The Army was the top employer of minorities, and millions of African Americans registered to serve during WWII.

James Gallagher's flight • March 2, 1949

A pilot from Melrose, Minnesota, became the first to fly a non-stop, around-the-world flight in a B-50 bomber dubbed the *Lucky Lady II*.

TRIVIA

Others to Know

Ingrid Bergman, Glen Miller

LET'S PARTY!

A chemist and inventor named Earl Tupper experimented with plastic and created a moldable and useful form of the substance that he developed into Tupperware. Though initially a financial failure, a single mom named Brownie Wise came up with the brilliant idea to market it through home parties. Tupper pulled her into the company.

CHARLES LINDBERGH

Charles Lindbergh, esteemed aviator, and his wife Anne Morrow Lindbergh moved abroad to escape the American media after the trial of their son's murderer. They visited Germany several times and were impressed with Nazism, particularly its nationalism and its impact on the Germany economy, military, and people. Lindbergh was even given the Service Cross of the German Eagle for his contributions to aviation in 1938. When violence in Germany escalated, they returned to the U.S. in 1939. From that point forward, they led the isolationist and anti-war efforts, believing Germany would end the war. An anti-Semitic speech given in 1941 ended his popularity, and the bombing of Pearl Harbor in December of that year pulled the U.S. into WWII.

"I felt like the moon, the stars, and all the planets had fallen on me."
— **Harry S. Truman** commenting on his ascendance to the presidency when talking to reporters.

As a result of an extremely rare genetic mutation called Alexandria's Genesis, **Elizabeth Taylor** had striking violet eyes. Many people with Alexandria's Genesis have 20/20 vision for life.

Fast-food Faves

In the 1940s, a Californian burger joint introduced a new concept to the American public — the **"drive-through."** This restaurant was called In-N-Out and is still around today.

Slinky

1943 - This toy was accidentally invented by Richard James, a mechanical engineer working to create a spring to use on ship equipment. James and his wife, Betty, dubbed the invention a Slinky and marketed it as a novelty toy.

UFO

People's fascination with UFOs began after WWII, when the U.S. began experimenting with rocketry. The first instance of a well-known UFO sighting was when a businessman named Kenneth Arnold claimed to have seen nine objects flying over Mount Rainier in 1947. He said they raced "like saucers skipping on water," and newspapers mistook his meaning and said they were shaped like saucers. Viola! The origin of the term "flying saucer."

Innovations of this period:
Cheerios • M&Ms • Slinky
atomic bombs • computers
Polaroid cameras • Tupperware

House Un-American Activities Committee

The House of Representatives established the House Un-American Activities Committee (HUAC) in 1938. Its objective was to investigate communist, fascist, and other leftist organizations. Those suspected of involvement in these groups were subpoenaed, interrogated, and pressured to name other members. Some believed the activities of the HUAC were protecting national security, and others dubbed it a partisan implement. During WWII, its main concern was the activities of Nazi sympathizers, but it shifted its focus to supporters of communism during the Cold War.

Balloon Bombers

During WWII, the Japanese attempted to bomb the American mainland using a surprising item — balloons. Thousands of these deadly balloons were fixed to explosives, released in Japan, and floated across the Pacific Ocean to the North American continent by way of jet streams. Only one of these balloon bombs proved to be fatal, killing a woman and five children in Oregon.

U.S.S. *Arizona*

The USS *Arizona* was one of the American battleships sunk during the bombing of Pearl Harbor. 1,177 sailors and Marines aboard the ship lost their lives. Today, the USS Arizona Memorial is situated above the sunken battleship off the coast of Ford Island and is accessible by boat. The architect who designed the memorial was Alfred Preis.

NEVER SURRENDER!

The Japanese honored duty and did not believe in surrender. As a matter of fact, some Japanese soldiers stationed at island outposts did not believe that WWII had ended and continued fighting. These men were called the "holdouts." Most famously, Lieutenant Hiroo Onoda continued waging guerrilla warfare in the jungles of the Philippines for almost 30 years before one of his old commanding officers ordered him to do so.

Future president **Ronald Reagan**, then a member of the Hollywood acting community and president of the Screen Actors Guild from 1947 to 1954, served as an FBI informant during the 1940s and 1950s. He was asked to provide the names of "pro-communist" members of the show business industry.

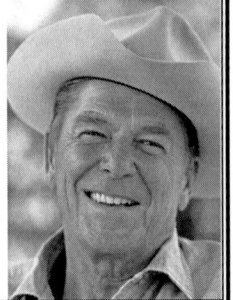

INDEX

PRIMARY RESOURCES

www.britannica.com

www.pbs.org

www.gilderlehrman.org

www.archives.gov

www.nationalgeographic.com

www.bbc.co.uk/history

www.loc.gov

www.tshaonline.org/home

www.si.edu

www.history.com

www.history.state.gov

www.smithsonianmag.com

https://nmaahc.si.edu

www.millercenter.org

www.nps.gov

www.ourdocuments.gov

www.time.com

MEET THE AUTHOR

"I was lucky to have the opportunity to compete in the University Interscholastic League and Academic Decathlon and recognize the impact these academic contests had on my life. It is a joy to remain a 'participant' in this corner of the academic world by cultivating my students' love of learning and competing."

— Keisha Bedwell

Keisha Bedwell is the director of Hexco's National History Bee personal coaching program and serves as an in-house researcher, writer, and editor specializing in social studies and writing-related contests. She holds a B.A. in both Psychology and History from Schreiner University and is a veteran tutor and writing coach. She brings a unique wealth of knowledge and insight to her work from her years of experience with coaching students of all ages and applies methodology gleaned from working in university tutoring centers and from studying and observing the workings of the National History Bee. In 2017, each of her students across the U.S. qualified for the History Bee's National Finals. When she's not writing or coaching, she enjoys traveling or spending time on the Guadalupe River with friends and her Australian Shepherd, Indie.

hexco